WYOMING
OREGON
IDAHO
Boise
Rocky Mts.
Cascade Range
Silvies
Columbia Plateau
Harney Basin
Lake Malheur
Snake River Plain
Lake Albert
Goose Lake
Warner Mts
Quinn
Bear
Wasatch Range
Great Salt Lake
Ogden
Black Rock Desert
Humboldt
Salt Lake City
Pyramid Lake
Ruby Mts
Great Salt Lake Desert
Reese
Reno
Great Basin
Provo
Carson
Utah Lake
Carson City
Sacramento
Lake Tahoe
Sevier
San Francisco
Valley
Mono Lake
Escalante Desert
Colorado Plateau
UTAH
Owens
NEVADA
ARIZONA
Death Valley
Amargosa
CALIFORNIA
Las Vegas
Mojave Desert
Lancaster
Mojave
Palmdale
Victorville
San Bernardino Mts
Los Angeles
Imperial Valley
Salton Sea
San Diego
Mexicali
Sonoran Desert
MEXICO

To all horses everywhere who suffer

the injustices of unnatural confinement . . .

Please enter . . .

*Paddock
Paradise*

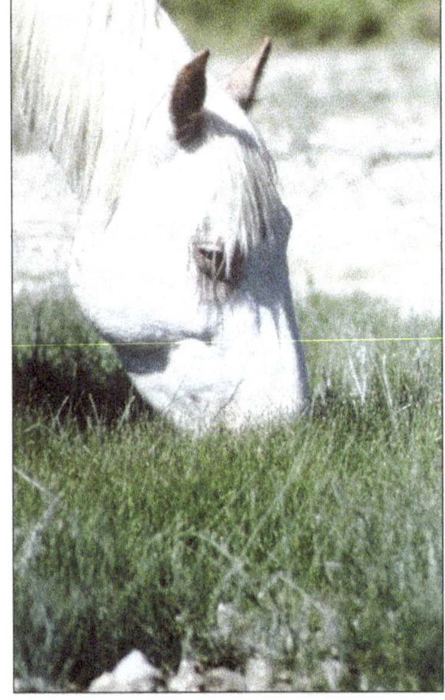

LESSON FROM
THE WILD
§
*Equine and bovine,
and occasional mule
deer and antelope,
are complementary
feeders and do not
compete aggressively
for available forage.
Each "stays to its
own" and go there
own way.*

with barbed wire, and entrance through the mountain pass is interrupted by a large cattle guard. Each year wild horses step accidentally into these "grates" where they become foot bound and panic stricken. What follows is death by trauma, and horse owners familiar with these devices can easily appreciate the terror experienced by horses caught in them. Our group of wild ones, quintessential survivalists, have learned to jump the grate, but it is still risky business.

Once inside the valley, they stay to their track and "ride the rim". All about, equine and bovine, and occasional deer family (mule deer and antelope), share the range. They are complementary feeders and, according to some researchers, do not compete aggressively for available forage.[1] For the most part, each "stays to its own" and goes its own way. We can use other complementary feeders to help control unwanted grass growth (a laminitis trigger) in Paddock Paradise — hence, another potentially invaluable "lesson from the wild".

First stop in Lost valley is "Sand Flat". Actually, it is more of a "dust flat" in certain spots than sand. This is because wild horses exploit this natural resource for personal ("self") grooming by means of rolling behavior. Countless generations of wild horses have visited to roll in this same area. In the process, the soil has been pulverized into a fine dust. While the textural "luxuriousness" of this natural "grooming powder" provides an enjoyable rolling medium, I wonder if there aren't veterinary implications as well — such as contributing to their characteristic vibrant and healthy coats? And perhaps protecting the skin against biting insects?

LESSON FROM
THE WILD
§
*While the textural
"luxuriousness" of this
natural "grooming powder" provides an enjoyable rolling medium, I
wonder if there aren't
veterinary implications
as well contributing to
their vibrant and
healthy coats?*

Whatever the case, in anticipating this favorite spot, our herd moves quickly to see who gets in line first!

Other wild horse herds from outlying areas may also enter the valley with an eye to this dusting station — converging simultaneously, as though it were pre-planned. In so doing, each will keep an acceptable distance from the next, according to the spheres of intolerance of the alpha stallions, At Sand Flat, "competitive" bands will take turns

---

[1] Ibid., Marlow et al.

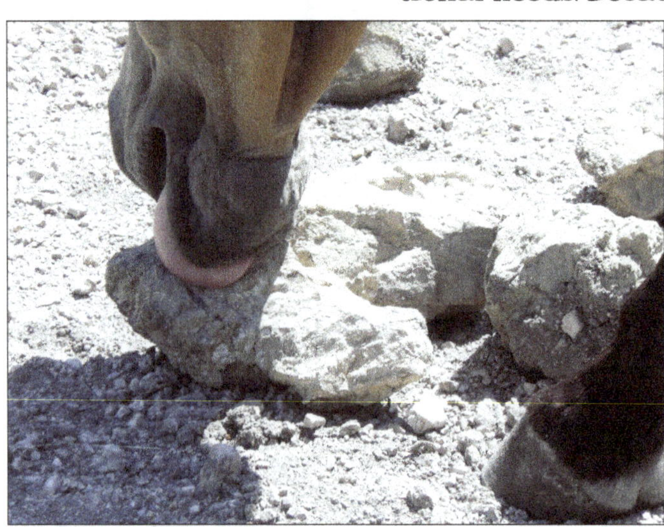

The Natural Horse: Lessons from the Wild (1992)

Horse Owners Guide to Natural Hoof Care (1999)

Founder — Prevention and Cure the Natural Way (2001)

Guide To Booting Horses for Hoof Care Professionals (2002)

Paddock Paradise: A Guide to Natural Horse Boarding (2006)

The Natural Trim: Principles and Practice (2012)

The Healing Angle: Nature's Gateway to the Healing Field (2014)

Laminitis: An Equine Plague of Unconscionable Proportions (2016)

Training Manual: ISNHCP Natural Trim Training Program (2017)

WYOMING
IDAHO
OREGON
Boise
Cascade Range
Columbia Plateau
Snake River Plain
Rocky Mts.
Harney Basin
Lake Malheur
Silvies
Lake Albert
Warner Mts.
Goose Lake
Quinn
Bear
Wasatch Range
Great Salt Lake
Ogden
Salt Lake City
Black Rock Desert
Humboldt
Great Salt Lake Desert
Pyramid Lake
Reese
Ruby Mts.
Provo
Utah Lake
Reno
Carson
Great Basin
Sacramento
Carson City
Lake Tahoe
Sierra Nevada
Walker
Sevier
Escalante Desert
San Francisco
Mono Lake
Owens
Death Valley
Amargosa
NEVADA
Colorado Plateau
UTAH
ARIZONA
CALIFORNIA
Las Vegas
Mojave Desert
Lancaster
Mojave
Palmdale
Victorville
San Bernardino Mts
Los Angeles
Salton Sea
Imperial Valley
San Diego
Mexicali
Sonoran Desert
MEXICO

*To all horses everywhere who suffer
the injustices of unnatural confinement . . .*

*Grazing behavior
is a slow, mouth-
to-the-ground,
eat-n-go affair
along the track*

graze in the Spartan landscape, and moving the band to-wards the next "event". What do they eat? The answer is that we know very little about the wild horse diet — indeed, until qualified researchers (e.g., Great Basin biologists, botanists, and geologists) enter wild horse country to make a systematic study, this invaluable "lesson from the wild" will remain a great mystery. We do know from studies of their hooves that it appears to be a "founder free" diet. And much of that diet appears to be range grasses and grass-like plants, and probably a wide variety of high desert type legumes. Some researchers have reported that wild horses spend roughly half their daily lives eating![1]

Hours may pass by as the nibbling here and there continues. On warm days, grazing may give way to periods of rest and relaxation at midday (#3/Track). Horses may lay down to sleep. In the safety of the family circle, such sleep behavior is commonly divided between those who remain awake and vigilant, and those reposed in muscle-twitching deep sleep. In a very emotionally moving experience in early 1984, I joined family members in a "cat nap", when I was suddenly aroused from my stupor by a young foal, who, unbeknownst to me, had laid ("collapsed" is

[1]Marlow, et al.

LESSON FROM
THE WILD
§
Grazing behavior is a slow, mouth-to-the-ground, "eat and go" affair along the track. Never meandering, and seldom at a dead standstill, movement is always directed towards finding fresh graze and moving the band towards the next "event".

LESSON FROM
THE WILD
§
Much of their diet appears to be range grasses and grass-like plants, and probably a wide variety of high desert type legumes.

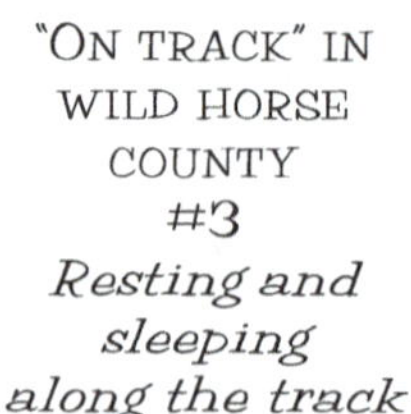

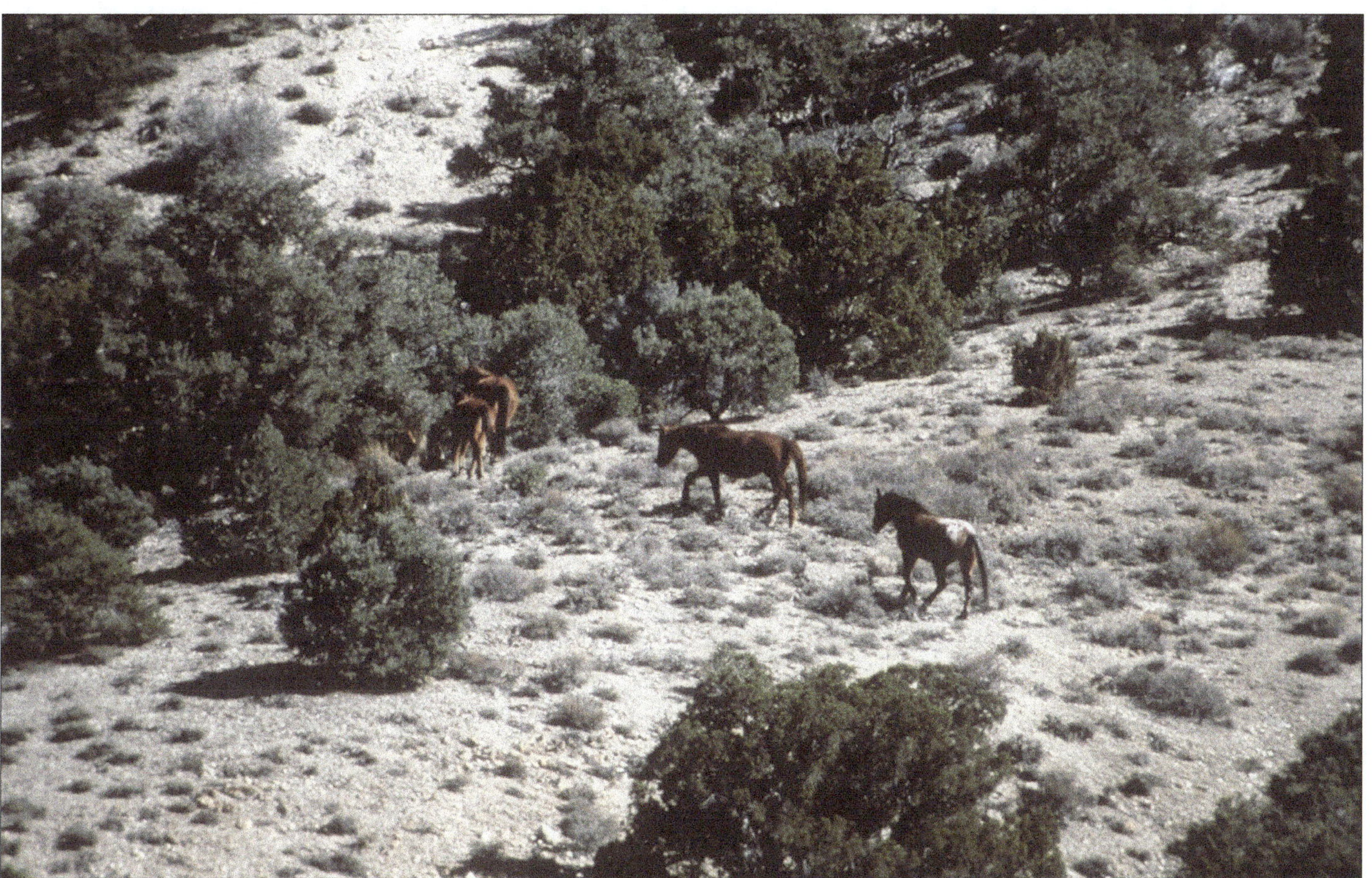

Chapter 1

"ON TRACK" IN
WILD HORSE COUNTY
#8
Suddenly, as we are
leaving the water
hole, a bachelor
stallion makes a
daring move to steal
one of the alpha
stallion's mares.

"ON TRACK" IN
WILD HORSE COUNTY
#7
[FACING PAGE, TOP]
*Stare down
in Paradise.*
—

[FACING PAGE, BOTTOM]
*Harem mares await
with outcome of stallion
rivalry with character-
istic indifference.*

alpha stallion's mares (*above*). He assumes a head down, ears-pinned-back body posture to intimidate his intended prize to leave the alpha's harem. But the alpha stallion, who himself had been momentarily occupied in a rear-guard action to keep yet another bachelor stallion at bay in a brilliant visual confrontation (*facing page, top*), quickly takes the field. In a flash he vigorously confronts this young foe as his harem mare rests nearby in sleepy indifference (*facing page, bottom*). The offender gives way without a fight, and returns to his satellite bachelor band. Such is the life of the "alpha Romeo", who forever must be on guard to protect his bevy of "Juliets".

§
THE GATE LEADING
TO OUTER PADDOCK

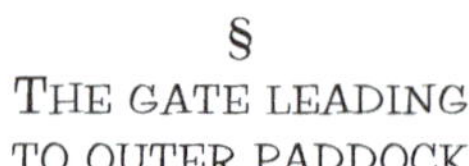

The "95—5 Principle"

Over the years I have listened to many arguments against natural boarding (i.e., why it can't work), one being that it is unrealistic, if not impossible, to get horses to move vigorously and sufficiently enough to do them (and their hooves) any good. Commonly: "I would have to ride my horse 30 miles a day to get him and his hooves looking natural. And who has time to do that?" I'm not sure how this purported "lesson from the wild" managed to take hold in the minds of so many horse owners, but the premise is fallacious and riding one's horse that much every day is actually unnecessary and probably harmful. Besides, who has time to do that anyway?

In fact, while wild horses may move that distance (usually less) in a given day, the majority of the time or "distance traveled" is spent walking, eating, and resting. In other words, horses spent most of their daily time engaging in "ordinary" behaviors (see "Lessons From The Wild" chart, p. 67) while on track. Riding, due to the fact that the horse is carrying the weight of a human, constitutes "extraordinary" behavior. While more definitive research on the subject of band behavior is badly needed to give clarity here, it was my observation in wild horse country that movement based on ordinary behavior constituted about 95 percent of their locomotive energy expended; extraordinary behavior only 5 percent, or less. This ratio of ordinary-to-extraordinary behavior is what I call the 95—5 Principle.

The 95—5 Principle helps us to interpret the relationship of the various behaviors which may take place within, and outside of, Paddock Paradise. Due to the nature of the track's construction, which favors ordinary behavior, I recommend that all extraordinary behavior take place outside Paddock Paradise. How this works exactly is easier to explain later after we've put the track together.

The good news here, according to the 95—5 Principle, is that, your horse only has to walk, eat, and sleep most of the time (his 95 percent quota) to develop a healthy body and beautiful naturally shaped hooves! A mere fraction of the time (his 5 percent quota) is spent engaging in vigorous behavior (movement), and at that, you don't really need to

grasses, the latter known to cause life-threatening laminitis — one of the deadliest killers and lamers of horses known today. In other words, by filling in the previous diagram a bit, we have something like this:

Paddock Paradise has a sturdy perimeter fence to contain the horses. It may be forested and planted in lush green grasses, as is the case here with this 5 acre tract— a deadly founder trap until Paddock Paradise changes everything.

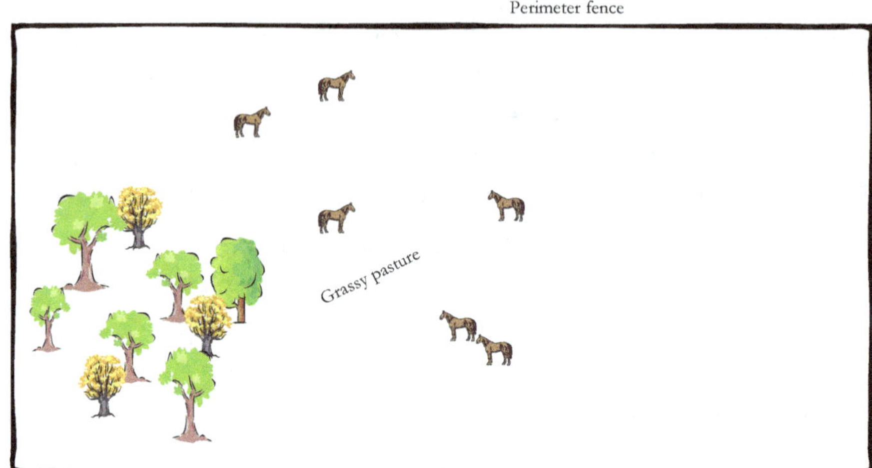

Obviously, we can't leave our horses stranded in there with this kind of threat! Ah, but we can, and this is where Paddock Paradise comes in. The first thing we want to do is create a second fence line *inside* the perimeter fence. This will be an electric fence, and we will place it approximately 10 to 15 feet away from the perimeter fence. Now, the horses are contained within two fences: a sturdy, stationary perimeter fence and an inner adjustable electric fence:

Creating "the track"

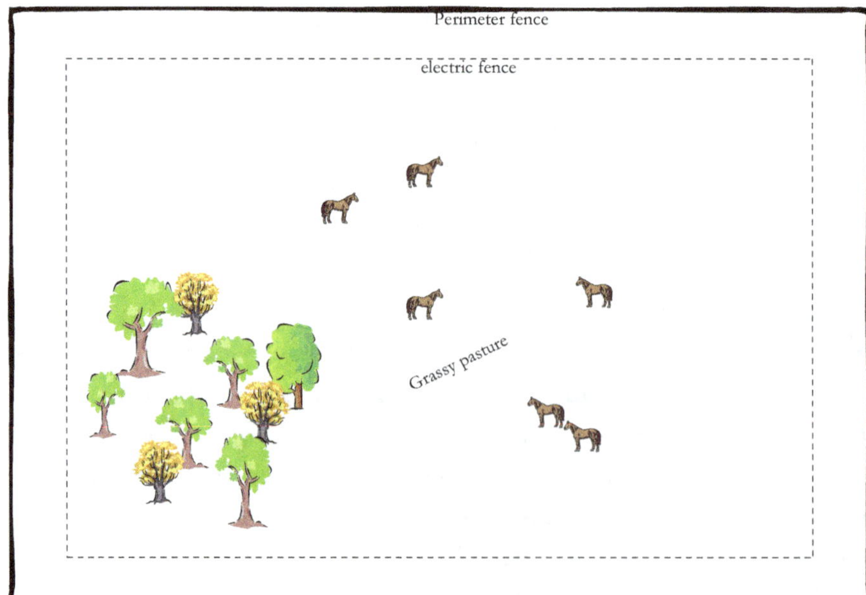

stimuli that correspond to the natural behaviors listed in the chart posted at the beginning of this chapter. The discussion that follows provides general guidelines for doing this, and these you should be able to adapt readily to your specific plot of land, regardless of its size or shape.

On the next page (*overleaf*) is a "master template" that corresponds to the discussion. I've added numbers that cross-link the discussion to the diagram. You'll want to refer often to it, but bear in mind that you will probably create a different look and track than what you see here. Chapter 4 gives an example of a "real life" paddock, which incorporates only a fraction of the possibilities recommended here (the owners did not have the benefit of this book when they created it), yet the horses are doing very well on track, and their owners are delighted.

On this note, let's start creating our track beginning with diet, since food, along with curiosity, are going to be foremost on our horses' minds.

Diet and Feeding Behavior

The first regimen of stimuli should relate directly to the horse's most pressing survival need, one nearly always present in his mind due to the nature of his digestive tract: diet. While research of the wild horse diet and feeding behavior is still forthcoming, there are basics we can apply to Paddock Paradise with good results.

It may come as a surprise to many horse owners, but horses naturally spend most of their time not resting, but eating — and eating on the move, seldom stationary in one place as is common with too many domestic horses unnaturally confined. Studies of wild horses I've cited earlier, corroborate my own observations that horses spend over half their daily lives feeding. And that figure increases during the winter, due to the diminished availability of forage on many winter

95-5 Principle

The ordinary Behaviors.

Apollo (monarch alpha) stands guard as his family members nap and sleep nearby at the AANHCP Paddock Paradise.
§
Chance (buckskin) is sound asleep next to his sister at the rolling site.

comforting scent of one another, or to simply lay about without pressure in quiet repose. I have fallen into comforted deep sleep myself on more than one occasion in this familial setting with the sounds, smells and sights of equine wildness all around me.

Horses love to sleep. And in the wild, they lay down to do this. But it always seems that one is left standing, rear hoof cocked, a sentinel at half-sleep. Come night, family bands, two or more together (including a bachelor band), will camp on an open ridge top, plain, or forest meadow. And so it was on my very first night ever among them, camp was set, by the alpha mare and stallion, and, taking their cue, I decided this was as good a time as any to get some shut-eye myself. Laying down in my sleeping bag, I peered into the stars above waiting for the first shooting star to streak the sky, a habit I acquired among them and

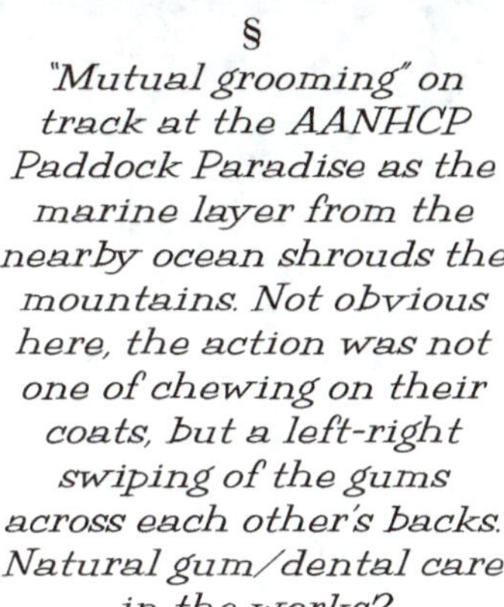

another in the open elsewhere, preferably on high ground. Your horses may choose to camp elsewhere, in which case, enlarge those areas — always just room enough to fit everyone in there together comfortably. That electric fence is meant to be moved as necessary to "best fit" your unique Paddock Paradise.

Reproductive and Foaling Behavior

I decided to group reproductive and foaling behaviors under the "extraordinary" classification of the 95-5 Principle. The stress and strains of breeding, and the struggles of the newborn foal to gather and collect himself within minutes of birth to join his family on track, are nothing less than extraordinary. This discussion should be of interest to horse breeders, or anyone with a mare ready to foal, because Paddock Paradise provides the ideal environment for reproductive and foaling behaviors.

When mares enter estrus, and assuming that breeders have targeted specific mares and stallions for procreation, I recommend that a given breeding stallion and his mares (to be bred) be placed on one track, and all other males removed to a second track (e.g., a bachelor band). If more than one stallion is breeding, then they also should be situated on their own tracks and with their respective mares. These kinds of divisions, or separations, occur in the wild, and therefore, apply in Paddock Paradise. (Multi-track systems are discussed further later in this chapter.) The exception to the foregoing would be when alpha and sub-dominant breeding stallions are "buddies" and prefer to be on the same track, rather than separated in a multi-track configuration. This occurs in the wild too,[1] and should be facilitated in Paddock Paradise with discretion. Breeding in all cases may take place on track, or, in combination with "turnouts" off-track; I can't see that it will make any difference.

From the moment of birth, newborn foals should live their lives on track, moving with the normal "flow" of movement established by the alpha mares and alpha males (if present). Within hours of birth, foals are ready to

---

95-5 Principle

—

The extraordinary Behaviors.

Facing page

—

Shadow of internal electric fence casts its long shadow down an empty track pocked with hollow hoof prints. As in wild horse country, Paddock Paradise keeps horses moving naturally.

---

[1]Ibid., *TNH*, p. 23-26

lry and arid.

www.ingramcontent.com/pod-product-compliance
Lightning Source LLC
Chambersburg PA
CBHW081420210726
48464CB00020B/1335

WYOMING
OREGON
IDAHO
Boise
Cascade Range
Columbia Plateau
Snake River Plain
Rocky Mts.
Silvies
Harney Basin
Lake Malheur
Lake Abert
Goose Lake
Warner Mts.
Quinn
Black Rock Desert
Humboldt
Bear
Great Salt Lake
Ogden
Salt Lake City
Wasatch Range
Great Salt Lake Desert
Provo
Utah Lake
Pyramid Lake
Reese
Ruby Mts.
Sierra Nevada
Reno
Carson
Carson City
Sacramento
Lake Tahoe
Great Basin
Sevier
San Francisco
Walker
Mono Lake
Escalante Desert
Owens
NEVADA
Colorado Plateau
UTAH
CALIFORNIA
Death Valley
Amargosa
ARIZONA
Las Vegas
Mojave Desert
Lancaster
Mojave
Palmdale
Victorville
San Bernardino Mts
Los Angeles
Imperial Valley
Salton Sea
San Diego
Mexicali
Sonoran Desert
MEXICO

Please enter . . .

*Paddock
Paradise*

obviously curious, will avoid us at all cost, scurrying to move out of our sight, and anxiously awaiting signs of our departure, In some wild horse ranges, cougars — natural predators of the mustang — stealthily take up their residence, coming out only to strike the horse herds with lightning speed. They prey upon foals with which to nourish their own young waiting in hidden dens.[1] In minutes, the attack is over and the prey is swiftly drug away, leaving no vestige that the event ever occurred. This pressure is ever-present in the wild horse mind, and band movements accordingly assume specific formations to minimize the danger of being caught off guard and vulnerable — another invaluable lesson from the wild that I will return to later. Yet, too, the skilled feline hunters avoid us, and the unwitting human visitor who does not know their signs, would never know they are ensconced from view in their dens nearby.

To find the wild horse, moving within his family bands, we must find water in his arid homeland. It is scarce. But once located, and if we are patient and take up positions slightly to the side, sooner or later the bands will arrive to

[1]A mountain lion requires 8 to 10 pounds of meat per day to survive. Its diet consists of deer, elk, porcupines, small mammals, livestock, and pets. Generally a lion prefers deer. Experts tell us a lion kills one deer every 9 to 14 days. (*Information compiled from U.S. Department of Agriculture, Wildlife Services, San Antonio, Texas, and Montana Fish, Wildlife and Parks, Helena, Montana*)

LESSON FROM THE WILD
§
Band movements assume specific formations to minimize the danger of being caught off guard.

"ON TRACK" IN WILD HORSE COUNTY
At the water hole

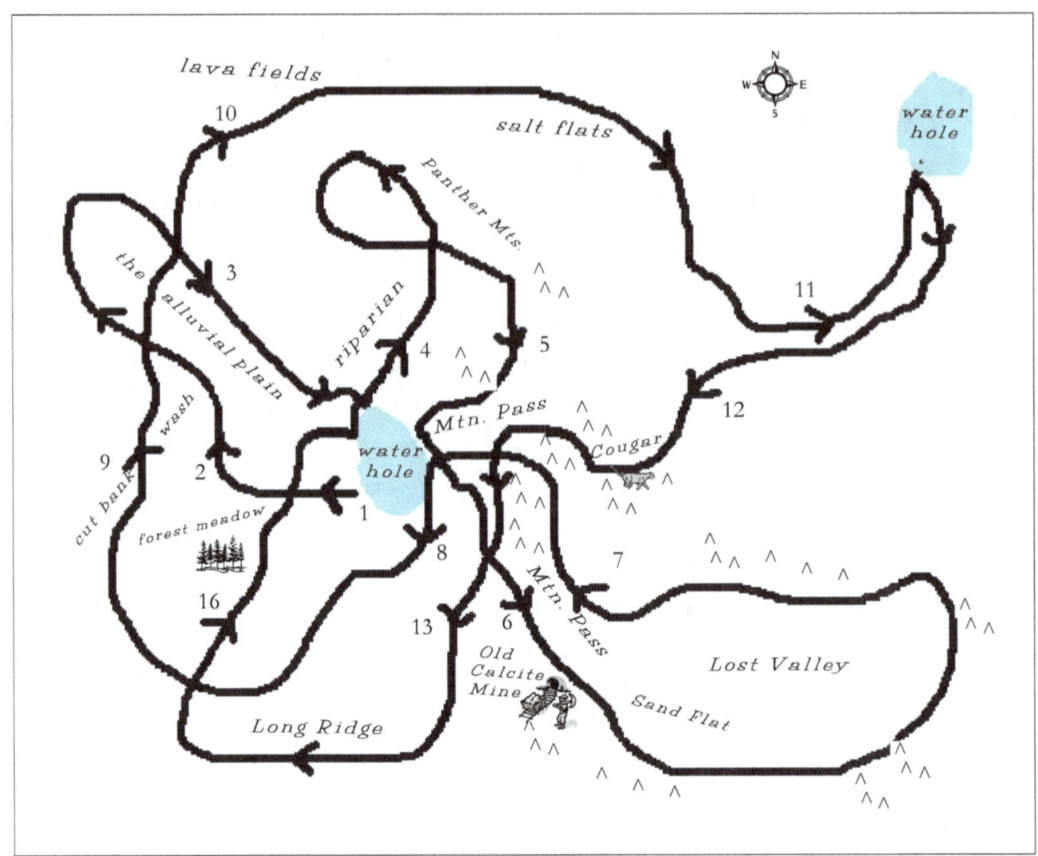

LESSONS FROM
THE WILD
§
*"On track" in a
typical Great
Basin wild horse
home range.*

LESSON FROM
THE WILD
§
*Their home ranges
are distinct areas
in which they
roam along well
defined paths.*

Sound confusing? Perhaps a little, but the point I wish to make here is that *wild horse society is comprised of family groups, never isolated individuals.*

Second, their home ranges are distinct areas in which they roam along well-defined paths or "tracks" as I now call them in relation to Paddock Paradise.[1] To the uninitiated human eye, one would readily conclude that band movements are random, and that the actual home range is without "boundaries" in the mind of the horse. But neither is the case at all, and, thus well-defined space and structured movement through it comprise yet another invaluable "lesson from the wild".

In 1984, I asked a BLM Wild Horse Management Specialist to help me draw a representation (*facing page*) of a typical Great Basin wild horse home range. At the heart of the home range are one or more water holes. All band

[1]2014 update: I will clarify this distinction between "tracks" and "paths" later in Chapter 3. Within the Paddock Paradise natural boarding model, paths are created by the horses themselves *within* the tracks which we create for the horses. In this interpretation, the two, therefore, are not the same. In fact, within a given track (wild or Paddock Paradise), there may be multiple paths forged by the horses.

LESSON FROM

THE WILD

§

*Horses at the water
hole during warm
months will often
roll in the dirt, if
not in the pond, in
order to muddy up
their coats. This is a
rolling behavior and
constitutes an im-
portant adjunct to
Paddock Paradise.*

ducted, and a definitive text written.[1] Nevertheless, these
are enough to get us going with the essential basics of Paddock Paradise. As more research comes forth from the
field, I will refer readers to those "lessons from the wild"
too.

As we begin, horses at the water hole, particularly during warm months, will often roll in the dirt, if not in the
water, in order to muddy-up their coats. This is "rolling behavior" and it constitutes an important "lesson from the
wild" and, thus, is another vital dimension to life in Paddock Paradise.

Mindful of being targets of the ubiquitous cougar, and
feeling the soft pangs of hunger, our herd now moves
briskly from the water hole at the trot to an open alluvial
plain — a sparse food packet of vital dry bunch grasses, the
mainstay of the wild equine diet. Coming to a walk it is
time to eat (#3/Track). Grazing behavior is a slow, mouth-
to-the-ground, "eat and go" affair along the track. Never
meandering aimlessly, and seldom at a dead standstill,
movement is always directed towards finding seasonal

[1] Of interest is a recent 1990's study by the National Park Service: *Feral Horse
Distribution, Habitat Use, and Population Dynamics in Theodore Roosevelt Na-
tional Park* by Clayton B. Marlow, Associate Professor of Animal and Range Sci-
ences; Leonard C. Gagnon, Associate Professor of Animal and Range Sciences;
Lynn R. Irby, Associate Professor of Fish and Wildlife Management; and Matt A.
Raven, Adjunct Assistant Professor of Agricultural and Technology Education.

Temperature and weather conditions will dictate how far wild horses venture from the vital water holes. If a given track is viewed as a dynamically expanding and contracting space, the area within it shrinks with the dry, hot summer months — as bands hug the water holes — and expands commensurately with the arrival of cool fall temperatures, In years of drought, wild horses have been known to venture into outlying ranches and urban communities to seek water (*above*); conversely, in severe winters marked by food shortages in the home range, they will again leave their tracks to enter the same alien haunts to graze lawns and shrubbery just to survive. In effect, new tracks are "laid" and the boundaries of the home range expand.

In the same way that thirst regulates the degree of track movement away from the water hole, so does the relative availability of forage and other vital nutrients, stallion rivalry, and pressure from predators, impact the *velocity* or speed of movement on a given track. Such pressure on the home range will cause bands to increase or decrease the quickness of their movements. Such are the forces of adaptation. A more plentiful grazing ground, for example, will absorb more attention from the band, thereby slowing it down on the track, than a sparsely vegetated one. Briefly, then, the vicissitudes of equine life in the wild regulate by necessity every dynamic — from concentration to velocity — of natural movement on the track.

LESSON FROM
THE WILD
§
The vicissitudes of equine life in the wild regulate by necessity every dynamic, from density to velocity, of natural movement on the track.

*"Mutual grooming" has
an important ritualistic
place in bonding be-
tween horses as well a
deterrent to aberrant
behavior stemming
from isolation*

physical proximity is — whether by herd instinct, monarch stallion — entirely in keeping with their nature.

Our herd has had its fill, and before leaving the valley
it is time to relax and engage yet another important pas-
time — grooming (#7/Track). In the wild, as among domestic horses, grooming may be personal or "mutual" with two
or more partners chewing on each other simultaneously.
The latter is quite the sight, an "open field" that may en-
compass just about every external body part that can be
mouthed by one's grooming partner! I've wondered if it is
more an expression of familial bonding, a way to pick a
fight (*overleaf, pages 36-37*) or outright hedonism. Perhaps
it is all three.

Another observation I would like to make involves
grooming the lower leg, which I first noticed in close proximity at the BLM's Litchfield Corrals near Susanville,
California. Literally, their legs may be yellow-coated with
bots, of which they chew upon like candy and ingest.
Which raises the question: if wild horses are eating them
(along with their dung — coprophagous behavior), and they
are healthy, then why do horse owners spend billions on

The situation continued on for the next four years until the owners sold out and closed the ranch. But I had learned a lot in the meantime. First, that the wild horse model could be adapted to domestic hoof care. Second, that the natural trim had both preventive and healing value. And third, that naturally trimmed horses could also be ridden barefoot. The Peruvian trainers demonstrated the latter perfectly to my satisfaction. Even then I was aware that the dirt and pavement they rode over wouldn't even begin to challenge the hooves worn by our wild ones.

Still, I noticed also that even though my trims generated handsome hooves, they still didn't resemble the much tougher and quite elegant hooves one sees in the wild. Characteristically, wild hooves have extremely short toe walls, descended heel bulbs which endure ground contact passively, and relatively (by industry standards) high "angles-of-growth" (e.g., toe angle) even though the heels are comparatively short to non-existent when contrasted with domestic hooves. Eventually, I learned that these differences cannot be attributed to the hoof work, no matter how good it is, but to the lack of natural wear driven by the horse's instincts — in other words, behavior. (For a detailed discussion on the features of the wild horse foot, see my other written works.[1])

As time went by, I began to speculate that natural wear may only arise from natural behavior. such as we see in the wild — behavior that we seldom see among domestic horses. And to a lessor extent, from the effects of environment. I was pretty much stumped on this dilemma, when another opportunity presented itself that brought me closer to the vision for Paddock Paradise.

🐎

A 20,000 acre "horse rescue" ranch (1985)

Of the many visitors who came to the Paso ranch each year to purchase horses, was a young lady whose family owned and operated a huge cattle ranch in the coastal mountains further to the east. Of interest to me was that

> "But I had learned a lot in the meantime. First, that the wild horse model could be adapted to domestic hoof care. Second, that the natural trim had both preventive and healing value. And third, that naturally trimmed horses could also be ridden barefoot."

[1] Go to my website (www.jaimejackson.com) for details, and also Star Ridge Publishing (www.star-ridge.com) to order copies of my, and others, works on the subject of natural hoof/horse care.

WILD HOOVES AT
LITCHFIELD, CA
(2005)
§
". . . after several
weeks or so of idle-
ness, their hooves
began to deteriorate
from the exemplary
form I had seen in
the home range."

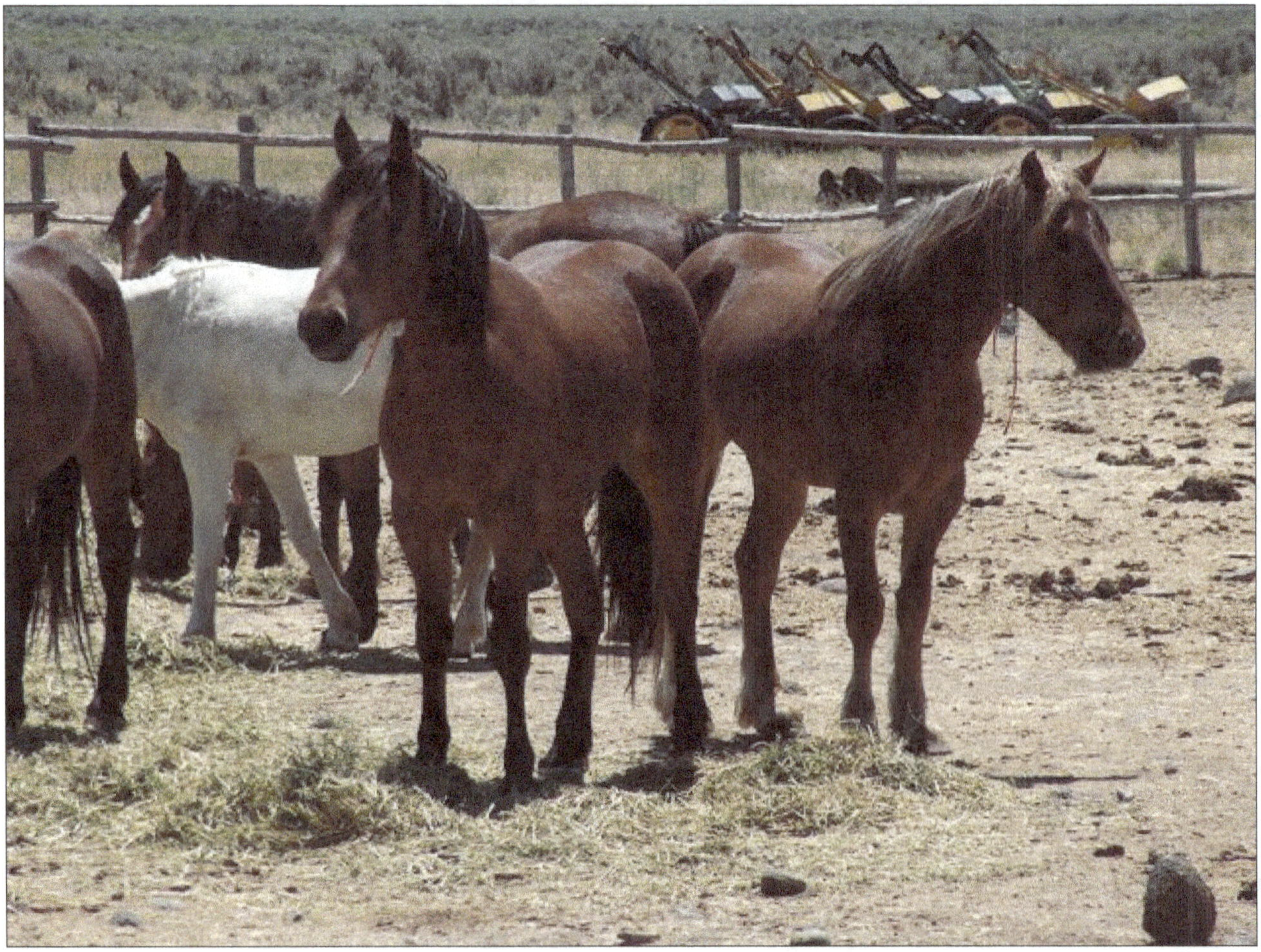

Customarily, horses are thrown whatever amount of
hay, grain, supplements, and so forth, we think they will
need for the day, usually in one, or at most, two feedings a
day. The horse is left to stand right there and eat what he
can. Depending on how much and what is provided, as
well as competition pressure from other horses, he may eat
it all at once or take a break (but to do what?) now and
then. This won't work in Paddock Paradise, and, fortunately, the construction of the track makes it easy to feed
a much better and more natural way.

What we want to do is spread the feed, particularly the
hay, around the track at regulated intervals. [Time to go
to the "Paddock Paradise Template", see *Overleaf, #1*]. The
idea is to space the hay so that the horses will keep moving. If we place too much in one spot, or in only one location, we will encourage "camping". Camping (discussed
later) is okay, but it shouldn't be feeding behavior based. I
would liken this to the opportunistic "greener pastures"
syndrome. Once introduced, our horses, either from curiosity or hunger, will begin to explore the entire track. As
each new hay "nugget" is discovered, they will quite readily want to move to the next, and before they finish what
they've started. Indeed, competition for forage from fellow
band members will help drive this syndrome. So, the pressure is on everyone to get going to eat. And it's good for
them. The alternative, gluttony — eating "super-sized"
meals in one place — is, to my thinking, a prescription for
indolence and colic.

Of course, it is nearly impossible for me to figure the
spacing for you, because it will depend on the number of
horses on track, how much you decide to throw per pile,
how many piles you decide to throw, and the size of the
track itself.

You may be asking yourself, how much hay should I
put out? There should be enough hay placed so that the
horses will never finish what is given to them in a day's
time, or whatever time interval you decide to feed by. As
mentioned earlier, I also recommend feeding a variety of
hays — not just one. Who wants to eat just one thing? And
who can survive eating just one thing?

So, scanning the entire track (PP Template), you will

Overleaf
§
*Template for
Paddock Paradise*

#1
—
PP Template

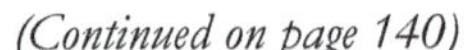

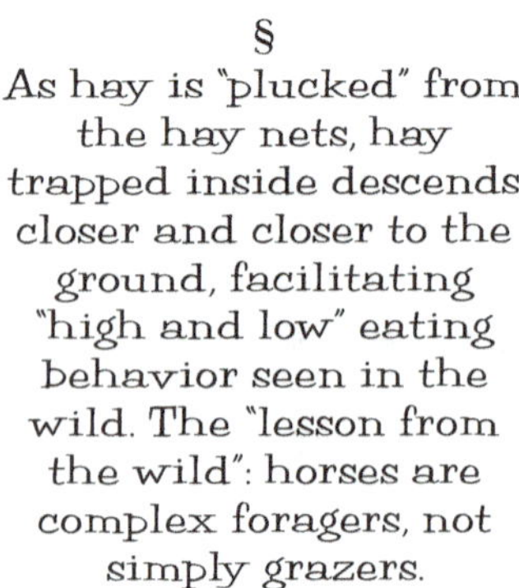

§
As hay is "plucked" from the hay nets, hay trapped inside descends closer and closer to the ground, facilitating "high and low" eating behavior seen in the wild. The "lesson from the wild": horses are complex foragers, not simply grazers.

(Continued from page 108)

after *Paddock Paradise* was published, countless horse owners have taken the concept and made it work for their horses in a range of biomes. This is what I had hoped for.

The reader is invited to the new Paddock Paradise website (www.paddockparadise.net) to see what horse owners around the world are doing with this important concept. So go check it out! Many photographs and videos pepper the ongoing dialogues (in many languages!) as people share ideas and continue to develop their tracks. Indeed, the very concept of Paddock Paradise so resonates with the highest ideals of "natural boarding" that the sky is the limit in what might be done. With the wild horse model to keep us all in check and serving, as it does, as a vast resource for ideas, it really comes down to human ingenuity to make the most of the "lessons from the wild".

If you are new to the Paddock Paradise concept, and perhaps this book is the first you've heard of it, then I encourage you to think of your horse and what it can do for him in the best of ways. None of us has to own horses. So, to my way of thinking as an advocate, it is incumbent upon each of us to do what is best, humanely so, for our

Paddock Paradise

"Our three horses are enjoying their new 'paradise'. They have lost weight, gained endurance, begun exhibiting increased happy herd behaviors AND their bare feet look wonderful. We've had the perimeter of two acres on track since March 12 and we're already working on more. Thank you for another great idea." (Tennessee)

"First of all thank you for your wonderful book — it answers so many of the questions and problems that have been in my head now for the last 2-3 years. So excited what a brilliant plan." (United Kingdom)

"I ordered your Paddock Paradise book last Sunday and it arrived midweek. By the time my husband got back from out of town on Friday pm. I had my paddock planned. It took me a day to convince him, but now he is also buying into the idea on the basis that it will be less work for him. Plus we will be able to have some 'pretty green pasture' in the off track area. He has always wanted 'photogenic pastures'. We are adding on to our indoor arena, so the timing was perfect. We have a tad bit less than four acres for the pasture, but we do have some great hills that will really work their muscles. And I swear our largest 'crop' in Wisconsin is ROCKS. I will no longer have to pick them out of the pasture." (Wisconsin)

"I will make sure that everyone will know about your books and your site! We are looking forward to helping our poor pony who is foundered. We can't wait to use your methods on our stallion, too. Thank you for writing these books and making them easy to understand for the normal layperson." (Great Lakes)

The Natural Horse: Lessons from the Wild (1992)
Horse Owners Guide to Natural Hoof Care (1999)
Founder – Prevention and Cure the Natural Way (2001)
Guide To Booting Horses for Hoof Care Professionals (2002)
Paddock Paradise: A Guide to Natural Horse Boarding (2006)
The Natural Trim: Principles and Practice (2012)
The Healing Angle: Nature's Gateway to the Healing Field (2014)
Laminitis: An Equine Plague of Unconscionable Proportions (2016)
Training Manual: ISNHCP Natural Trim Training Program (2017)

Paddock Paradise

A Guide to Natural Horse Boarding

Jaime Jackson

Star Ridge Publishing

Table of Contents

WYOMING
OREGON
IDAHO
Boise
Cascade Range
Silvies
Columbia Plateau
Harney Basin
Lake Malheur
Snake River Plain
Rocky Mts.
Lake Albert
Goose Lake
Quinn
Warner Mts.
Bear
Great Salt Lake
Ogden
Wasatch Range
Black Rock Desert
Humboldt
Salt Lake City
Great Salt Lake Desert
Pyramid Lake
Reese
Ruby Mts.
Provo
Utah Lake
Sierra Nevada
Carson
Reno
Great Basin
Carson City
Sacramento
Walker
Lake Tahoe
Sevier
San Francisco
Mono Lake
Escalante Desert
Colorado Plateau
UTAH
Owens
Death Valley
NEVADA
Amargosa
ARIZONA
CALIFORNIA
Las Vegas
Mojave Desert
Lancaster
Mojave
Palmdale
Victorville
San Bernardino Mts
Los Angeles
Salton Sea
Imperial Valley
San Diego
Mexicali
Sonoran Desert
MEXICO

*To all horses everywhere who suffer
the injustices of unnatural confinement . . .*

Please enter . . .

*Paddock
Paradise*

Welcome to *Paddock Paradise*!

The "paradigm" for creating a new system of natural horse boarding proposed in this book has been long in coming. I began thinking seriously about natural and humane living conditions for domestic horses over 20 years ago, when I left wild horse country for the last time. For those readers who are unfamiliar with my previous written works, my adventures in the world of our truest "natural horses" — America's wild, free-roaming horses — laid down the foundations for a lasting personal philosophy and practice regarding the general natural care of horses. My first book about them, *The Natural Horse: Lessons From the Wild,*[1] was the most immediate extension and application of that philosophy and experience. *TNH* is a broad treatise about equine life in the wild and a call to find ways wherein we can apply its vital "lessons" to the care of their domestic cousins. Years later, *The Natural Trim: Principles and Practice* (2012) answered that call at the horse's foot, providing my own and others' interpretations and applications of the wild model in the new and now burgeoning frontier of "natural hoof care".

The delay in writing *Paddock Paradise* since leaving wild horse country in 1986 can be attributed to my lengthy efforts at bringing the "natural trim" before the farrier and veterinary communities, gaining acceptance of the wild horse model by horse owners (since until that is established, this book would be moot), and availability of new electric fence technology.

---

[1] Published by Northland Publishing (AZ) in 1992 and reissued by Star Ridge Publing in 1997 as *The Natural Horse: Foundations for Natural Horsemanship.*

Paddock Paradise takes us above and beyond the hoof, if not the animal himself, and addresses how horses may be confined naturally based on the wild model, The "call" of *Paddock Paradise* is also an urgent one. Unnatural systems of boarding (e.g., close confinement, green pastures and diet), so natural hoof care practitioners have learned the hard way, undermine our efforts to shape and stimulate sound, naturally shaped hooves. Unnatural boarding systems also are not conducive to healthy and sound bodies and minds. While it is recognized by most that horses are, as a species, animals of prey, we have in our ignorance created systems of confinement that are actually suitable for animals of predation. For example, close confinement, — "life in a cave" (cf. stall or paddock) so to speak — favors the cougar, a natural enemy of the horse in wild horse country. The cougar requires such an existence (walls close around him, and preferably in the dark) to feel and be "normal". But the same living conditions imperil the horse, turning him into a lazy, neurotic, and weakened paradox of his true natural self — a prime candidate for lameness. He naturally must be free to move constantly, and everything depends on it for his mental and physical well-being and soundness.

From wild horse country, I always knew would come the true foundations for creating any "honest to life" natural boarding system for domestic horses. But as with everything else concerning their lifestyle (e.g., how we can adapt the model to the feet), the challenge has been to find a way to translate those "lessons from the wild" into viable practices horse owners and professionals could act upon for the good of horses in their care. This book, *Paddock Paradise* is my answer to that calling.

From 1982 to 1986, I traveled among wild horses to study their "Way". How they live, as well as the nature of their environment (or "home range"). I was a farrier then, and, not surprisingly, I focused (at first) mainly on their feet. But being the sort of person I am — heavily inclined towards "no baloney" holistic thinking — it wasn't long before I began to observe and appreciate the supreme significance of matters above and beyond the hoof. Indeed, that

the very lifestyle of the animal, driven by natural behavior, lay at the bottom of optimum hoof form and health: their freedom, as it were, to choose where they will or will not go, to eat what their instincts tell them they should and should not be eating, and to behave like real horses, It is their world entirely, and the deleterious influences of domestication are by and large unknown among them.

From these observations, I came to realize that the bottom-line "difference" between wild horses and domestic horses could really be reduced to simple terms of optimal health and soundness. By wild horse standards, domestic horses are neither healthy nor sound. They are frail parodies of their wild counterparts, and few horse owners and professionals are even aware of this. And they are this way because of us. This is a serious indictment of our management practices, but it is not without corroborative data coming from within the horse-using community itself. According to Walt Taylor, co-founder of the American Farriers Association, and a member of the World Farriers Association and Working Together for Equines programs:

> Of the 122 million equines found around the world, no more than 10 percent are clinically sound. Some 10 percent (12.2 million) are clinically, completely and unusably lame. The remaining 80 percent (97.6 million) of these equines are somewhat lame . . . and could not pass a soundness evaluation or test. [American Farriers Journal, Nov./2000, v. 26, #6, p. 5.]

These grim statistics reflect directly on unnatural boarding and hoof care practices. *Paddock Paradise* aims to open the door to the missing freedom and lifestyle of their natural world by situating and propelling the horse forward in an unprecedented environmental configuration that, holistically speaking, both stimulates and facilitates natural movement. A healthy animal is the result. And because the hoof is adaptively cross-linked to this nexus of natural behavior and environment — it too is restored to its native integrity and soundness. Arguably, Paddock Paradise, brought functionally to full vision, may mean the end of hoof care as we know it today, with the horse "trimming his own feet" naturally. And, I hope, the promise of reversing the alarming levels of unsoundness cited by Taylor above.

Surprisingly simple in its architecture (albeit perhaps a strange sight to the human eye accustomed to conventional paddock and pasture confinement systems), Paddock Paradise puts horses in a simulated natural environment. Its core intent is to stimulate natural movement and socialization patterns that are essential to a biodynamically sound horse. As an example, Paddock Paradise is inherently the perfect place for the healing or prevention of navicular syndrome and laminitis, today's greatest killers of domestic horses. Too, it readily enables natural feeding patterns that are consistent and integral

EQUINE INTERNMENT CAMP — THE PLIGHT OF MOST DOMESTIC HORSES
§
We have ironically created predator confinement systems that favor mountain lions, not our horses, and certainly not healthy horses as exemplified by the wild horse model.

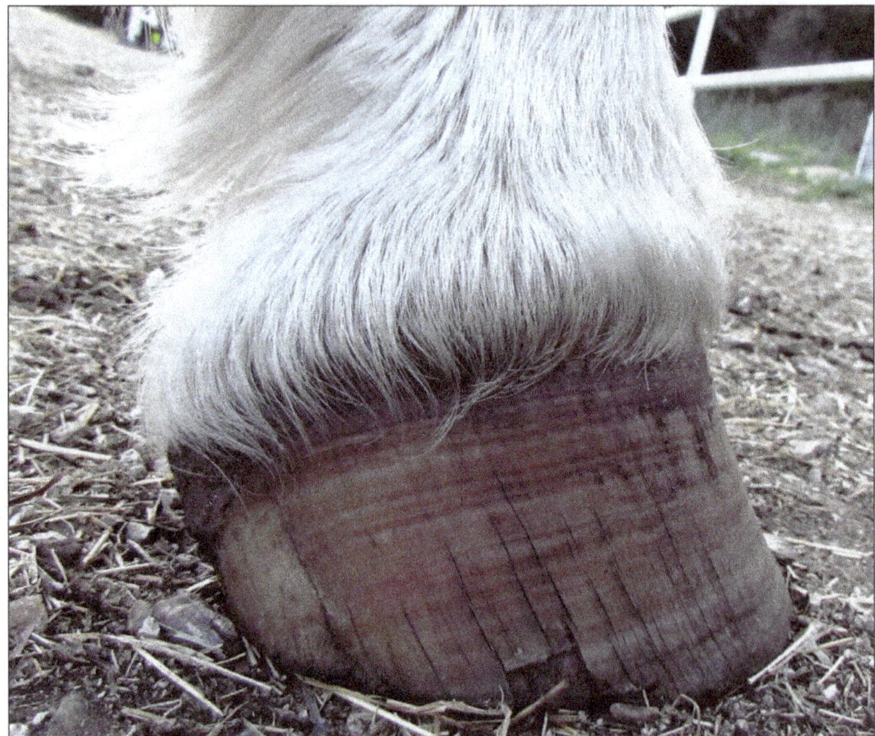

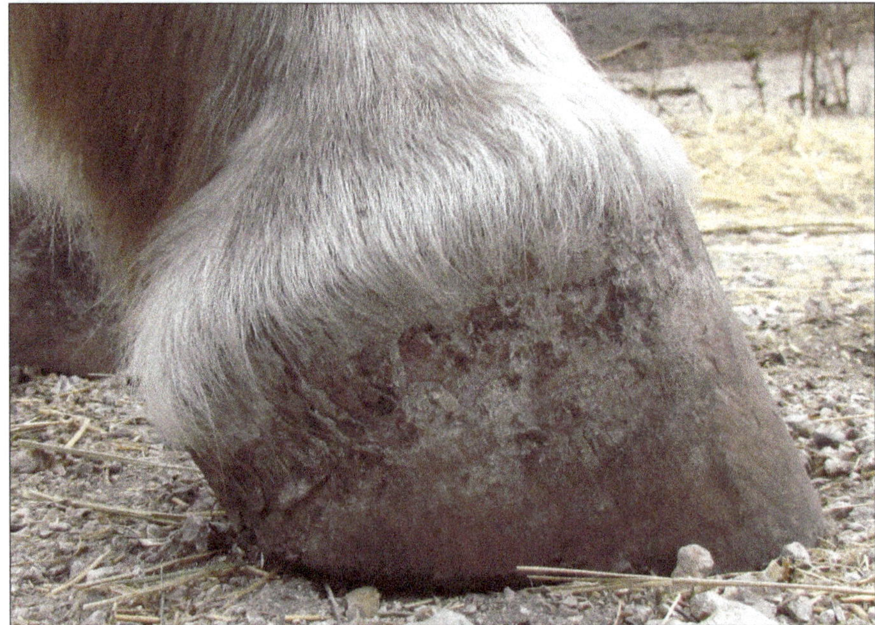

The power of Paddock Paradise and a reasonably natural diet was demonstrated at the AANHCP Field Headquarters when a 14 year old mare with clubfoot and a history of chronic laminitis was put on track. Within months, all laminitic stress rings and splits in the hoof walls (*above*) completely disappeared (*below*), and hoof angles modulated dramatically into natural ranges. She is completely sound, moves 24/7 over challenging terrain, and her hooves, which dull my rasp with each swipe, are as tough and durable as any I witnessed in wild horse country. Paddock Paradise delivers — so I encourage every horse owner to go for it!

with the horse's digestive system. And it facilitates the implementation of a safe (e.g., founder-free) diet in a controlable feeding environment.

Another benefit: because Paddock Paradise stimulates continuous natural movement, — tantamount to a perpetual "warm-up" session — it also prepares the horse for his rigorous equestrian duties. He is "ready to go" whenever he is needed, and he usually requires no additional prelimary warm-up at all. By way of contrast, horses standing listlessly around all day — the plight of most domestic horses — are always at risk of ligament, tendon, and muscle strain when they are put to use on short order with only brief warm-ups, if any at all. Horses optimally need a 24/7, on-going warm up, and Paddock Paradise delivers!

Countless other examples abound, as this book will reveal. But suffice it to say that the promise and intent of Paddock Paradise is always to deliver a naturally healthy and sound horse. Just like his wild cousin!

To truly grasp the underlying foundation for Paddock Paradise, indeed what it is all about and what we must do to create it, we must momentarily take leave of the domestic horse world and return to the wild. There, we will take note of its "lessons", harvest what we can from them, and with a little clever imagination and elbow grease, put them to work for our horses in Paddock Paradise — and right in our own backyards!

Jaime Jackson

Lessons From the Wild

TO LEARN FROM THE WILD HORSE, we must first find him. To find him we must know something of his world. Indeed, what shapes the horse's natural world? What is the nature of the environment to which he is so well adapted? How does he survive there — what is he doing exactly? And, very important,, what is it exactly about his life way that renders him so sound and healthy? These are the "lessons from the wild" we are in search of, and now we must find him to teach us.

Stepping into wild horse country, we are immediately a taken by its vast and spectacular landscape. It is "Big Sky" country.

View from my nearby base camp, central Nevada, 1984.

Perched atop any one of its mountain peaks or ridgelines, we are left breathless by the view, the eerie quiet, and the distinct smells of wildness. It completely, totally envelops our senses the moment we enter their world. Such is the raw and sensual power of wild horse country.

But long before we find them, they — through a unique system of communication native to their species — are probably aware of our presence. As are the myriad other wild life that inhabit the same rangelands. Most, save the

obviously curious, will avoid us at all cost, scurrying to move out of our sight, and anxiously awaiting signs of our departure, In some wild horse ranges, cougars — natural predators of the mustang — stealthily take up their residence, coming out only to strike the horse herds with lightning speed. They prey upon foals with which to nourish their own young waiting in hidden dens.[1] In minutes, the attack is over and the prey is swiftly drug away, leaving no vestige that the event ever occurred. This pressure is ever-present in the wild horse mind, and band movements accordingly assume specific formations to minimize the danger of being caught off guard and vulnerable — another invaluable lesson from the wild that I will return to later. Yet, too, the skilled feline hunters avoid us, and the unwitting human visitor who does not know their signs, would never know they are ensconced from view in their dens nearby.

To find the wild horse, moving within his family bands, we must find water in his arid homeland. It is scarce. But once located, and if we are patient and take up positions slightly to the side, sooner or later the bands will arrive to

---

[1] A mountain lion requires 8 to 10 pounds of meat per day to survive. Its diet consists of deer, elk, porcupines, small mammals, livestock, and pets. Generally a lion prefers deer. Experts tell us a lion kills one deer every 9 to 14 days. *(Information compiled from U.S. Department of Agriculture, Wildlife Services, San Antonio, Texas, and Montana Fish, Wildlife and Parks, Helena, Montana)*

"ON TRACK" IN WILD HORSE
COUNTY
At the water hole

drink and bathe. Watering behavior is distinctive here, particularly in mountain lion ranges, where band survival is at stake under the pressure of feline predation. As animals of prey, wild horses are instinctively on high alert, and so their stay at the water hole must necessarily be to the point and as brief as possible, especially if young foals are among them. Staying too long in any one place, particularly the water hole where the cougar, too, knows they must come, is an invitation to slaughter. Even so, this is where we hope to pick up their trail, and, if all goes well, to "join up" and learn from them. Surrounding each family band is an "invisible bubble" of space that they do not like breached. Wildlife biologists call this the "sphere of intolerance" and it applies aptly to the wild horse. But if we are not too pushy, sooner or later they will begin to cautiously ignore our intrusions and allow us to come closer. Eventually we may follow them around as peripatetic students. A perfect way for us to learn![1]

Before following along with the wild ones just arriving at the water hole, let's look at two key features of wild horse society that will help us to understand the general nature of their movements through their home range.

First, they are not rogues, but move as horse families in distinct formations. Typically, there is an alpha or monarch stallion stationed at the rear of the band, urging forward movement as necessary, and fending off competitive males in the area. Then there is his favorite mare — generally the alpha female— leading most band movements from the front. Also, commonly, there are one or more other harem mares subdominant to the alpha mare. And, too, the young offspring, always at or near the mother's side. Finally, and kept by the alpha stallion at an acceptable distance away from his herd, a pack of stallions not yet aggressive enough to claim their own females. Possibly also nearby are one or more "allied" harem bands, led by the alpha stallions which are subdominant to the "principal" monarch described above.

LESSON FROM
THE WILD
§
Surrounding each family band is an 'invisible bubble' of space that they do not like breached.

LESSON FROM
THE WILD
§
Wild horse society is comprised of family groups, never isolated individuals.

---

[1] It is upon this system of learning, borrowed from the ancient Greeks, that the mentorship training session of the AANHCP (www.aanhcp.net) was founded.

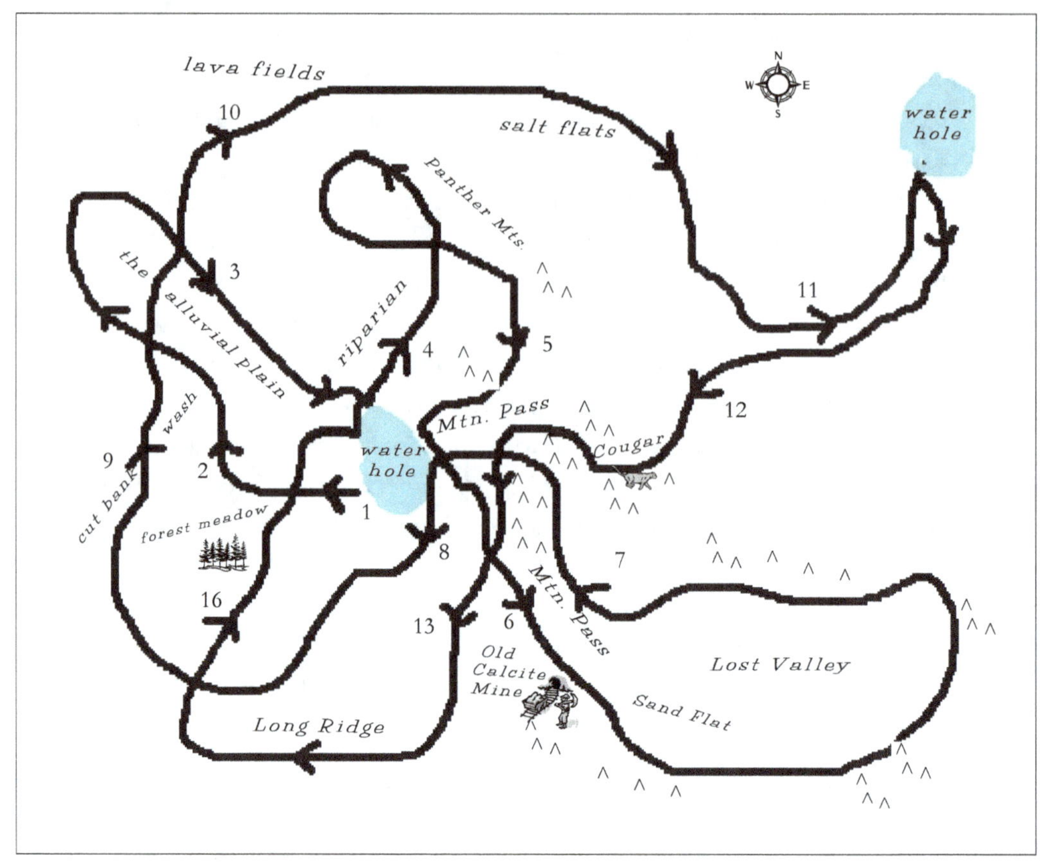

Sound confusing? Perhaps a little, but the point I wish to make here is that *wild horse society is comprised of family groups, never isolated individuals.*

Second, their home ranges are distinct areas in which they roam along well-defined paths or "tracks" as I now call them in relation to Paddock Paradise.[1] To the uninitiated human eye, one would readily conclude that band movements are random, and that the actual home range is without "boundaries" in the mind of the horse. But neither is the case at all, and, thus well-defined space and structured movement through it comprise yet another invaluable "lesson from the wild".

In 1984, I asked a BLM Wild Horse Management Specialist to help me draw a representation (*facing page*) of a typical Great Basin wild horse home range. At the heart of the home range are one or more water holes. All band

[1] 2014 update: I will clarify this distinction between "tracks" and "paths" later in Chapter 3. Within the Paddock Paradise natural boarding model, paths are created by the horses themselves *within* the tracks which we create for the horses. In this interpretation, the two, therefore, are not the same. In fact, within a given track (wild or Paddock Paradise), there may be multiple paths forged by the horses.

movements center around these. The tracks leading away from the water holes, sooner or later turn back to them, depending on temperature and thirst. Interestingly, one or more home ranges may overlap — often at the waterhole. This fact will play a key role in how we later design Paddock Paradise.

BLM managers in the early days of the Reagan Administration learned quickly that wild horse families "on track" do not like to leave their home ranges. Horses would cling tenaciously to their familiar tracks, despite efforts by government wranglers on horse back and helicopter to drive them away to distant loading areas. At the slightest mitigation of pressure from the wranglers, bands would turn back into their haunts like iron filings to magnets. It became apparent that setting "traps" within or very close to their domains was far more efficient. This vital "lesson from the wild" will be applied in the management of our projected Paddock Paradise: we will recognize that horses are basically "home-bodies" who relish familiar surroundings and familial routine.

Let's now "get on track" with our family bands who are restlessly preparing to leave the water hole (#1/map track) and look a little closer at their pathways through the homeland.

🐎

Chances are good that you will first be "greeted" by the alpha stallion, as seen in the photo at right taken in western Nevada. This is one of his many "jobs" — checking out intruders venturing into the homeland. Once he has accepted your presence, a general tolerance may be extended to move near his family herd (dominant family band, sub-dominant family band, bachelor band, etc.) on the track. So, away we go!

What follows by way of description represents just a few of the many possible behavioral "events" that occur on the homeland track. The better our picture of these natural behaviors, the better able we will be to provide similar opportunities within Paddock Paradise. A comprehensive study of the wild horse's lifestyle has yet to be con-

ducted, and a definitive text written.[1] Nevertheless, these are enough to get us going with the essential basics of Paddock Paradise. As more research comes forth from the field, I will refer readers to those "lessons from the wild" too.

As we begin, horses at the water hole, particularly during warm months, will often roll in the dirt, if not in the water, in order to muddy-up their coats. This is "rolling behavior" and it constitutes an important "lesson from the wild" and, thus, is another vital dimension to life in Paddock Paradise.

Mindful of being targets of the ubiquitous cougar, and feeling the soft pangs of hunger, our herd now moves briskly from the water hole at the trot to an open alluvial plain — a sparse food packet of vital dry bunch grasses, the mainstay of the wild equine diet. Coming to a walk it is time to eat (#3/Track). Grazing behavior is a slow, mouth-to-the-ground, "eat and go" affair along the track. Never meandering aimlessly, and seldom at a dead standstill, movement is always directed towards finding seasonal

[1]Of interest is a recent 1990's study by the National Park Service: *Feral Horse Distribution, Habitat Use, and Population Dynamics in Theodore Roosevelt National Park* by Clayton B. Marlow, Associate Professor of Animal and Range Sciences; Leonard C. Gagnon, Associate Professor of Animal and Range Sciences; Lynn R. Irby, Associate Professor of Fish and Wildlife Management; and Matt A. Raven, Adjunct Assistant Professor of Agricultural and Technology Education.

graze in the Spartan landscape, and moving the band towards the next "event". What do they eat? The answer is that we know very little about the wild horse diet — indeed, until qualified researchers (e.g., Great Basin biologists, botanists, and geologists) enter wild horse country to make a systematic study, this invaluable "lesson from the wild" will remain a great mystery. We do know from studies of their hooves that it appears to be a "founder free" diet. And much of that diet appears to be range grasses and grass-like plants, and probably a wide variety of high desert type legumes. Some researchers have reported that wild horses spend roughly half their daily lives eating![1]

Hours may pass by as the nibbling here and there continues. On warm days, grazing may give way to periods of rest and relaxation at midday (#3/Track). Horses may lay down to sleep. In the safety of the family circle, such sleep behavior is commonly divided between those who remain awake and vigilant, and those reposed in muscle-twitching deep sleep. In a very emotionally moving experience in early 1984, I joined family members in a "cat nap", when I was suddenly aroused from my stupor by a young foal, who, unbeknownst to me, had laid ("collapsed" is

[1] Marlow, et al.

*In wild horse coun-
try, there are favor-
ite sleeping areas
away from perceived
threats, usually in
more open country
where predator
movement is more
readily detected.*

probably a more fitting description!) near my side, resting
her young head upon my legs. I had similar experiences
with snakes snuggling against me for warmth during night
campouts on track; so, in similar fashion, I simply laid
back to wait it out as a human pillow and comforter! In
wild horse country, there are favorite sleeping areas away
from perceived threats, both in open and not-so-open country where predator movement is more readily detected.
This is another important "lesson from the wild", and we
should make every effort to simulate the same sleeping
sanctuaries in Paddock Paradise.

Temperature and weather conditions will dictate how far wild horses venture from the vital water holes. If a given track is viewed as a dynamically expanding and contracting space, the area within it shrinks with the dry, hot summer months — as bands hug the water holes — and expands commensurately with the arrival of cool fall temperatures, In years of drought, wild horses have been known to venture into outlying ranches and urban communities to seek water (*above*); conversely, in severe winters marked by food shortages in the home range, they will again leave their tracks to enter the same alien haunts to graze lawns and shrubbery just to survive. In effect, new tracks are "laid" and the boundaries of the home range expand.

In the same way that thirst regulates the degree of track movement away from the water hole, so does the relative availability of forage and other vital nutrients, stallion rivalry, and pressure from predators, impact the *velocity* or speed of movement on a given track. Such pressure on the home range will cause bands to increase or decrease the quickness of their movements. Such are the forces of adaptation. A more plentiful grazing ground, for example, will absorb more attention from the band, thereby slowing it down on the track, than a sparsely vegetated one. Briefly, then, the vicissitudes of equine life in the wild regulate by necessity every dynamic — from concentration to velocity — of natural movement on the track.

Continuing along our roadmap, we see that our band has slowly returned to the starting point at the water hole, but now sets off in a northerly direction (#4/Track).[1] And what's this? Just above the water hole, our family herd has reached a small, delicate, spring-fed riparian oasis. These infrequent, high desert gardens provide just a mouthful or two of lush, tender graze for our equine party, before they hurriedly move on. Indeed, almost as if nature planned it that way, the mountain range just to the east is pocked by cougar dens. It is a danger zone, and while for months out of the year, mountain lions nearby descend to prey upon deer herds that migrate through this sector of the home range, the deer are now gone and our horse families are fair game. Just as well, the oasis is a mixed blessing for our family members, for a riparian area, like any lush body of green grass, may very well become a "laminitis trap" when frequented as an unrestricted resource.

On the hunt for forage, our herd now moves northward to the edge of a vast lava field. Later, on a separate track further north, they will move across this bed of razor sharp pumice — "nature's hoof care service" — and it is worth our consideration in mapping out the topography of Paddock Paradise. We will visit this in more detail later.

Turning back from the daunting volcanic moonscape, our herd instead nibbles its way to the east, where it will briefly ascend the northern flank of the stout Panther Mountains. (#5/Track). This unique mountainous rise just above the desert floor gives birth to

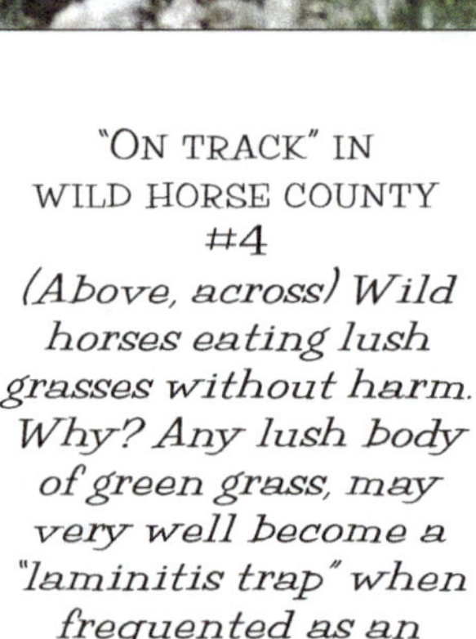

"ON TRACK" IN
WILD HORSE COUNTY
#4
(Above, across) Wild horses eating lush grasses without harm. Why? Any lush body of green grass, may very well become a "laminitis trap" when frequented as an unrestricted resource.

[1]How much time has passed, and how far have they gone, the reader may be asking. The answer is it will depend on the time of year and availability of forage. Horses may venture out 2 to 3 days without water in winter, but return once or more daily during the hottest months. This research has not been done yet in wild horse country.

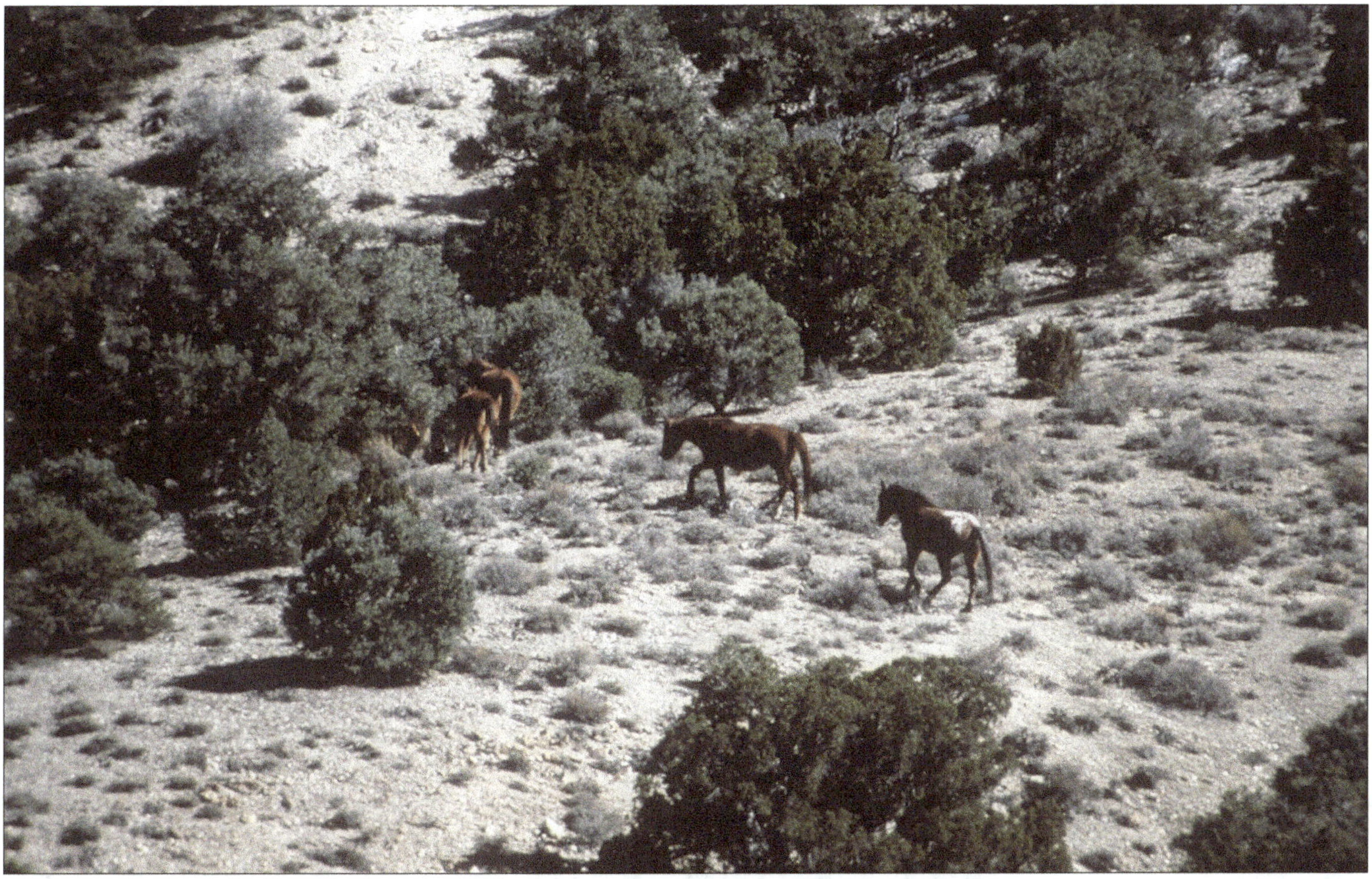

a panoply of unique forage — bark, herbs and leaves I was not able to catalogue, not being a botanist of the high desert biome. At higher elevations, particularly with forested slopes, the mountains also provide a cool respite from the intense heat of the lower alluvial fans. In my personal sojourns here, it has been my observation that their species seems not without an awareness and appreciation for the beauty that abounds here. At the risk of sounding anthropomorphistic, I am speaking of the eerie if not sleepy solitude wherein one can hear a pin drop, the soothing playful wind streams chiming upon the needles of the gnarly juniper stands, and the awesome panoramic vistas accorded at every outcropping. One wonders what is crossing the minds of the white stallion and his comrades on the page 29 as they indulge themselves in splendor 3,000 meters above the desert floor? If there is a "lesson from the wild" here, it is that we should make every effort to "dress up" Paddock Paradise in the simple name of natural beauty.

"ON TRACK" IN WILD HORSE COUNTY #5
Ascending the rocky, western flank of the Panther Mountains.

Moving southward upon the summit of Panther Mt., our family band nibbles here-and-there upon chamomile-like flowers and other herbs. In winter, there might be snow to consume too. Before long, however, as they sense the ubiquitous presence of the stealthy cougar, track velocity now begins to pick up. But soon the south end is reached, and the entire band spills down the mountainside, kicking and galloping, returning yet again to the favored water hole serving at the center of their lifestyle.

⭑

With thirsts quenched, we are off again. The new itinerary will lead us to the Old Calcite Mine above Panther Mt. Pass, through which we will cross over into Lost Valley. Prospectors opened the calcium carbonate fields before 1900, but long before then, since the days of the Conquistadors, wild horses had discovered the precious mineral deposits themselves. Our family members soon set to work, prying at the ground with their tough hooves to unearth the embedded white, chalky calcium deposits. A snowy white dust cloud soon looms above the herd as they whet their appetites by grinding the vital mineral with their teeth. This an important way — albeit unconsciously — that wild horses manage their own teeth while meeting important nutritional needs. It is, in my opinion, another vital "lesson from the wild" which, facilitated in Paddock Paradise, may aid or substitute the veterinary practice of rasping the dental arcades.[1]

Their cravings sated, our herd wastes little time in continuing its journey into Lost Valley. The latter is a sandy, grassy plain, shared by many cattle which are monitored by ranchers who lease these public lands. Deep wells have been drilled here and there, and the wild ones, much to the chagrin of many ranchers, use the surface watering troughs freely with their bovine counterparts. The valley is ringed

---

[1] The timing for this application in Paddock Paradise may be propitious. According to an article published in the *Equine Disease Quarterly*, "Numerous theories are being presented as to what is normal tooth structure, what abnormalities are correctable, and how much correction should be done. To date, no controlled documented studies have been presented to show the benefits of aggressive rasping of the dental arcades, especially to the table surfaces of equine teeth. R.D. Scoggins. "Evolution of Equine Dentistry", *EDQ*, Dept. of Veterinary Medicine, Maxwell H. Gluck Equine Research Center, University of Kentucky. Apr./2004., v. 13, no. 2, p. 3-4.

Sidebar:

LESSON FROM THE WILD
§
[FACING PAGE] Their species seems not without an appreciation for the beauty that abounds here.

LESSON FROM THE WILD
§
They grind the vital mineral (calcium) with their teeth … one way that wild horses manage their own teeth while meeting important nutritional needs. It may aid or substitute the veterinary practice of rasping the dental arcades.

with barbed wire, and entrance through the mountain pass is interrupted by a large cattle guard. Each year wild horses step accidentally into these "grates" where they become foot bound and panic stricken. What follows is death by trauma, and horse owners familiar with these devices can easily appreciate the terror experienced by horses caught in them. Our group of wild ones, quintessential survivalists, have learned to jump the grate, but it is still risky business.

Once inside the valley, they stay to their track and "ride the rim". All about, equine and bovine, and occasional deer family (mule deer and antelope), share the range. They are complementary feeders and, according to some researchers, do not compete aggressively for available forage.[1] For the most part, each "stays to its own" and goes its own way. We can use other complementary feeders to help control unwanted grass growth (a laminitis trigger) in Paddock Paradise — hence, another potentially invaluable "lesson from the wild".

First stop in Lost valley is "Sand Flat". Actually, it is more of a "dust flat" in certain spots than sand. This is because wild horses exploit this natural resource for personal ("self") grooming by means of rolling behavior. Countless generations of wild horses have visited to roll in this same area. In the process, the soil has been pulverized into a fine dust. While the textural "luxuriousness" of this natural "grooming powder" provides an enjoyable rolling medium, I wonder if there aren't veterinary implications as well — such as contributing to their characteristic vibrant and healthy coats? And perhaps protecting the skin against biting insects?

Whatever the case, in anticipating this favorite spot, our herd moves quickly to see who gets in line first!

Other wild horse herds from outlying areas may also enter the valley with an eye to this dusting station — converging simultaneously, as though it were pre-planned. In so doing, each will keep an acceptable distance from the next, according to the spheres of intolerance of the alpha stallions, At Sand Flat, "competitive" bands will take turns

---

[1] Ibid., Marlow et al.

"ON TRACK" IN
WILD HORSE
COUNTY
#6 - #7
*Resisting the pro-
pensity to
"disperse", family
members arrive
at Sand Flat,
where they will
roll and "self-
groom" in a
unique dust bath.*

§

*Dust rises like
smoke off the val-
ley floor as fam-
ily members com-
plete their rolling
session before
moving on from
Sand Flat.*

"ON TRACK" IN
WILD HORSE COUNTY
#6
Stallions sparing
in Lost Valley

accessing the premier rolling spots, the most dominant
bands seizing the area first. Close encounters may lead to
stallion "blufferies" (*above, facing page*), nipping and playful — and not-so-playful — sparring, and rarely even a full-
blown battle if mares happen to be in estrus. But this is an
important "grooming parlor", and true "fighting behavior" —
a real favorite among male horses — must wait until later
on another track to the north.

With the male theatrics and family rolling spectacles
behind them, our herd moves off along the southern rim of
Lost Valley. Bunch-type grasses abound here, as they do
everywhere in the valley, providing our horses with energy storage for the impending winter season. There is a
subtle temptation to disperse — that is, to fan out across
the plain where others can't compete for every mouthful
of grass. But the "herding" instinct for self-preservation —
again, the ubiquitous threat of the stealthful cougar — is
too powerful to tolerate dispersion. Nor would alpha stallions allow it. Whatever the centripetal force, the "lesson
from the wild" here is that keeping horses together in close

physical proximity is — whether by herd instinct, monarch stallion — entirely in keeping with their nature.

Our herd has had its fill, and before leaving the valley
it is time to relax and engage yet another important pas-
time — grooming (#7/Track). In the wild, as among domestic horses, grooming may be personal or "mutual" with two
or more partners chewing on each other simultaneously.
The latter is quite the sight, an "open field" that may en-
compass just about every external body part that can be
mouthed by one's grooming partner! I've wondered if it is
more an expression of familial bonding, a way to pick a
fight (*overleaf, pages 36-37*) or outright hedonism. Perhaps
it is all three.

Another observation I would like to make involves
grooming the lower leg, which I first noticed in close proximity at the BLM's Litchfield Corrals near Susanville,
California. Literally, their legs may be yellow-coated with
bots, of which they chew upon like candy and ingest.
Which raises the question: if wild horses are eating them
(along with their dung — coprophagous behavior), and they
are healthy, then why do horse owners spend billions on

parasiticides annually to treat their horses? It may be that in Paddock Paradise, if configured closely after our wild model, these chemicals may not be necessary or even desirable.[1]

❦

Our family herd once more moves through Panther Mountain Pass to return to the familiar water hole. They will drink their fill in preparation for a long, but important journey to a distant water hole frequented by many herds. The horses seem eager and their pace is quick, with considerable trotting along the way. It is a 25 mile sojourn, with a long and treacherous stretch across the vast pumice field we encountered on an earlier track. They will do it easily in a day.

But suddenly, as we are leaving the water hole, a bachelor stallion makes a daring move to steal one of the

[1]2014 update: our AANHCP paddock paradise has demonstrated over the past 3 years that such harsh parasiticides aren't necessary at all. Instead, we employ effective measures that leave and biodegrade dung on track.

"ON TRACK" IN
WILD HORSE COUNTY
#8
(Above) Youngsters are aroused from their naps as family bands prepare for the journey over Panther Mountain Pass and places beyond.

LESSON FROM
THE WILD
§
It may be that in Paddock Paradise, if configured closely after our wild model, horse worming may not be necessary or even desirable.

—

*[OVERLEAF]
"Aggravated assault"
Stallions doing what they love to do most!*

alpha stallion's mares (*above*). He assumes a head down, ears-pinned-back body posture to intimidate his intended prize to leave the alpha's harem. But the alpha stallion, who himself had been momentarily occupied in a rearguard action to keep yet another bachelor stallion at bay in a brilliant visual confrontation (*facing page, top*), quickly takes the field. In a flash he vigorously confronts this young foe as his harem mare rests nearby in sleepy indifference (*facing page, bottom*). The offender gives way without a fight, and returns to his satellite bachelor band. Such is the life of the "alpha Romeo", who forever must be on guard to protect his bevy of "Juliets".

Our family herd now skirts the base of Long Ridge (*facing page*), and soon reaches a massive cut bank, a gorge really, at which point they descend into a deep, eerie wash wherein they seemed to have been swallowed whole into the belly of the high desert biome. There is nothing to graze down in there, being principally composed of rock formations and sand. But here and there they stop to nibble at various mineral deposits embedded in the west wall of the gorge. One might never guess that such a circuitous excursion into such desolation would yield potentially valuable mineral supplements.

A half mile later, they reach the great alluvial plain from whence our journey originated. With little nibbling along the way, they traverse it in an hour heading generally northward. This is very "directed" movement, and band members understand that they are to keep moving. Twice they cross their earlier tracks (#2 and #3), and both alpha stallions defecate upon huge dung piles at each intersection before leaving the plain. Known as "stud piles", these are apparent territorial markers to let equine intruders know that they have entered an alpha stallions domain. The piles seem to signal: Beware!

Lava tubes

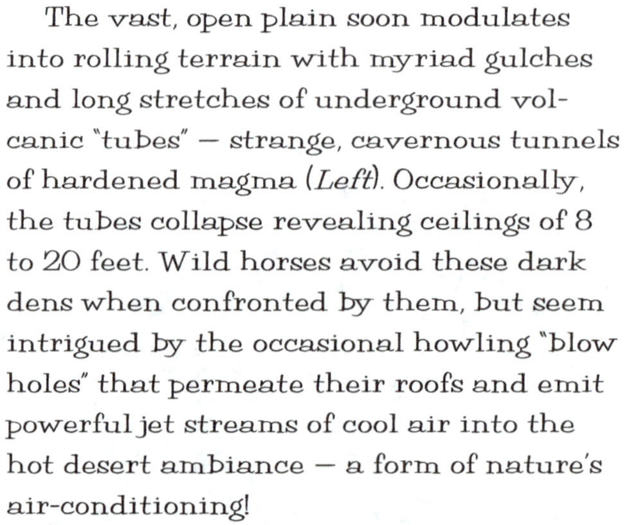

The vast, open plain soon modulates into rolling terrain with myriad gulches and long stretches of underground volcanic "tubes" — strange, cavernous tunnels of hardened magma (*Left*). Occasionally, the tubes collapse revealing ceilings of 8 to 20 feet. Wild horses avoid these dark dens when confronted by them, but seem intrigued by the occasional howling "blow holes" that permeate their roofs and emit powerful jet streams of cool air into the hot desert ambiance — a form of nature's air-conditioning!

Of interest to us are the immense beds of pulverized, sharp-edged, igneous rock from these extraordinary lava flows which carpet large areas of wild horse country. Our horses move over them effortlessly and without any apparent hy-

Collapsed lava tube

"ON TRACK" IN
WILD HORSE COUNTY
#16
At the base of
Long Ridge

persensitivity or deleterious effect upon their feet. This significant "lesson from the wild" tells us that the horse's foot is highly adaptable to even the most extreme terrain and most abrasive surfaces imaginable in the natural world. Recalling my own observations in my book, *The Natural Horse* (1992):

> The terrain in wild horse country is as diverse as the wildlife that often roams across it. The horses, whose hooves I examined at the [BLM's] Litchfield Corrals, were removed from high desert locations (woodland-brush biome) in northern California, Nevada, and eastern Oregon. Much of this land is similar. Typically, there are mountains (5,000 to 10,000 feet), small buttes (mesas), gently rolling hills, and broad alluvial plains. Rocks and boulders are scattered everywhere. The plains, where natural, are normally a mixture of firm soil and soft sand, interspersed with small volcanic rocks and a myriad of plant life and grasses.[1]

Moving eastward now, our family bands clear the lava beds and experience yet another dramatic change in the home range terrain. Briefly they encounter a small salt flat, or what is also known as a dry lake. Wild horse country is pocked with these geological "saline" sinks, the termini for ancient extinct rivers, which, thousands of years ago, formed inland lakes before drying up due to major climatic changes in the Great Basin. Our family bands, and other herds from nearby home ranges, utilize these flats as salt licks. The experience, while satiating their cravings for salt, also creates thirst. As quick as they arrived, then, they are off again to reach their next destination — a another water hole further east.

LESSON FROM
THE WILD
§
Immense beds of pulverized, sharp-edged, igneous rock from these lava flows carpet large areas of wild horse country. Yet, our horses move over them effortlessly and without any apparent hypersensitivity or deleterious effect upon their feet.

---

[1]Page 27.

As they approach within a mile of the water hole (#11/Track), our family herd is greeted by an unknown stallion from another home range (*above*). His mission is to challenge the dominant alpha stallion and "steal" one or more of his concubines. He is actually a harbinger of more strife to come, as the mares are coming into estrus and competitive stallions are driven by their hormones which compel them to sexual competition. Our dominant alpha stallion (below), surrounded by his curious offspring, takes the challenge to turn back the unwelcome

"ON TRACK" IN WILD HORSE COUNTY #11
A lone stallion arrives (above) to challenge our band's monarch (below) who attacks his adversary with great fury; in the battle that ensues, dung will fly fifty yards in every direction.

Wild horses gather at a waterhole in a Northern Utah HMA. Some five bands here suddenly gathered from separate home ranges to meet at this spot . . .

. . . when suddenly, in response to some circadian rhythm we humans cannot hear, they gallop off, soon separating once more into their native haunts.

intruder, while his bevy of females form a "mares' circle" to rest and ignore the commotion (*above*), also a defense formation used to protect the young when cougars threaten the herd. As fate would have it, our sub-dominant alpha joins in to help drive off the would-be Romeo, and the family band is soon "herded" onwards by the stallions towards the water hole.

At the water hole, many bands converge, as though on notice to do so at the same time. As many as 100 horses may be present, each band taking turns in order of relative dominance to avail themselves of the oasis in which they will stand, drink, roll, and bath. Some of the younger bachelor stallions cannot resist the temptation, and much hock and body nipping occurs in and around the water hole, not unlike during the "dust bath" we saw earlier on track.

The water hole interaction is an important time in the sexual selection of wild horse society. Young females leave or are driven off by their fathers to find their mates. Some older stallions are unseated by a younger generation, and older mares may elect to leave with a deposed senior. Or a more aggressive or astute male will simply de-throne an aging alpha male. A myriad of possibilities are at work, all of which, through a raw lifestyle of "survival of the fittest", strengthen the gene pool and perpetuate their species.

After considerable bluffing and fighting (both real and play), exchanging of mates, visiting and bathing, the "macro herd" dissolves and rejuvenated family bands retreat to their respective tracks and home ranges. As estrus comes full term, males and females breed until all are settled and a less restive pace is restored to the track.

⤤

On the last leg of our journey, the band must move through a perilous stretch of track. It is the eastern slope of Panther Mountain and cougars lie in wait. One of the mares bred 11 months earlier is ready to foal, and instinctively she will separate herself from the band to birth. The band remains close by, in patient vigilance, aware of the proximity of the feline threat. That night, as the family bands hug closely together, we hear the vocal trumpet-

LESSON FROM
THE WILD
§
*Breeding on track
is a natural
occurrence.*

ings of distant alphas calling out to each other. An exciting chorus in refrain ensues, ricocheting off the stark butte walls for miles, lasting for minutes. Indeed, each bellowing, which I have never heard among our compressed and repressed domestic horses, resembles a cross between the tuba and bugle. No doubt, the cougars lying in wait hear them too, and it is a sign that prey is near.

By morning, the foal has arrived and our family, one member stronger, hits the trail. The foal has no trouble keeping up with the pace. The rather peculiar looking hooves, not yet forged into the characteristic mature form worn by the adult's. are like "blank slates" ready to be pressed into natural form by the vicissitudes of equine life in the wild.[1]

The band soon arrives at the door of Panther Pass, and within an hour has safely reached the north-south corridor leading to Long Ridge, where an array of high desert legumes will be harvested.[2] On any given day, however, a cougar could have swept down upon the herd, perhaps while the latter is in repose, kill the foal instantaneously, and retreat with it into the hills to feed herself and her young. But today, the family herd is unscathed and moves forward apprehensively on track.

Descending Long Ridge, our families now enter a juniper and drought-resistant pine forest (#16/Track), which forms a kind of sylvan "hedge" between Long Ridge and the alluvial fan to the north. Within and winding through the forest and its intermittent meadows, is a very rare, year-round stream At one meadow, everyone stops to drink and nibble at the dry bunch grasses. In the forest, they strip bark from several trees, and it is thought that some of these barks may impart arsenic-like compounds that inhibit or prevent parasite infestation. This may be

---

[1] See my description of foal hooves in TNH (1992), p. 89.

[2] Some researchers have cited as many as 200 different legumes comprising ˜10% of the bulk diet. Consistent with my own field observations is the Hansen, et al. (see below) finding that the wild horse diet is comprised mainly of grasses and sedges, although altitude and regional biomes will cause shifts in eating behavior based on availability of specific forage. What this means is that the wild horse diet is far more adaptable and complex than most of us can begin to imagine. The university sector and equine feed industry must take to the field to research this vast gap in our knowledge. In Hansen's own words, "There is

another invaluable "lesson from the wild" in the natural care of our domestic horses. Indeed, is a safe, natural parasiticide awaiting our veterinary pharmaceutical industry to bring it forth from the wild?

The final leg of the track returns us to the water hole (#1/Track), from whence we began. From here, the journey will begin anew once more, Such is the calling of equine life in the wild. Its vicissitudes and circadian rhythms play to a genuine "circle of life".

❧

The Lessons Summarized

While not an exhaustive description of equine life in the wild, many of the "lessons from the wild' identified

LESSON FROM THE WILD #16
Wild horses naturally seek out forests, which form part of their home range . . . there is some speculation that the bark from some trees and woody plants deliver vital antiparasitic nutrients.

need for additional research on the food relationships of large and small herbivores . . . to simultaneously quantify food habits, food distribution, herbage production and herbivore populations by season" [R.E. Hubbard and R.M. Hansen, Colorado State University, *Diets of Wild Horses, Cattle, and Mule Deer in the Piceance Basin, Colorado*, JRM, 29(5), Sept. 1976]. See also: R.M. Hansen, R.C. Clark, and W. Lawhorn, Colorado State University, *Foods of Wild Horses, Deer, and Cattle in the Douglas Mountain Area, Colorado*, JRM 30(2), March 1977. And: R.M. Hansen, Colorado State University, *Foods of Free-Roaming Horses in Southern New Mexico.* JRM 29(4), July 1976.

here in the text and sidebars of preceding pages, will be enough to jump start our plans to create a natural boarding environment and lifestyle for our domestic horses.

In Chapter 3, I itemize the many behaviors discussed in this chapter in a chart adapted from my book, *The Natural Horse*. Our objective in that chapter will be to stimulate as many of these behaviors as we can, using the "lessons from the wild" just discussed — and others as new research from the field emerges to educate us. Study these lessons, the images, and the stories in this chapter — they are not irrelevant but represent the very core of Paddock Paradise.

Bringing the sounds and smells of wildness into Paddock Paradise need not be a daunting experience. While challenging, the endeavor can also be creative and enjoyable. And I am certain that our horses will welcome the opportunity to be what nature has always intended them to be, and so unwittingly they will be our greatest allies in the undertaking. Our objective, then, is to learn how the lessons should be applied to elicit the desired natural behavioral complex, exemplary health, and sound hooves we are seeking for our horses.

For years, I have wondered how we might simulate life in the wild for the domestic horse. There has been much incentive to figure it out, purely from the stand-

LESSON FROM
THE WILD
§
*Mules and burros
also lead lives on
track in wild horse
country, witness
the mare mule (3rd
from left) in this
family band.*

point of humane care. Countless horses founder each year in green pastures, which are not at all natural to the horse. Others become unhealthy and perish in both body and spirit from the deleterious influences of close confinement. Horses are not meant to live in caves like the cougar. Even in a paddock or pasture with no green grass to trigger laminitis, horses invariably just stand around or fail to move naturally. Unlike their wild cousins, they are listless and unmotivated.

So, what are we to do? Even though I spent 4 years visiting our wild ones and studying their ways, the vision for conceiving a Paddock Paradise for our domestic horses continued to elude me. I thought at the time, surely all the information that I needed to resolve the conundrum lie before me. As it turns out, I was right. But nature hadn't fully prepared me yet to see it. The next chapter explains the breakthrough that rendered this book and our model for Paddock Paradise possible.

In Search of A Natural Boarding Model

Peruvian Paso Breeding Ranch (1984)

Not two years had passed since I entered wild horse country when, through a series of intermediaries, I was asked by the manager of a Peruvian Paso breeding operation in Northern California to take a look at their horses' feet with an eye to having me become their "resident farrier". There were 350 to 400 Pasos there at the time, a mix of breeding stallions, mares, and young ones. One stallion in particular had chronic laminitis (founder) and the previous farriers had no luck with him. While many of the horses had minor hoof issues that really needed attention, it was this stallion that motivated his owner to bring me to the ranch. Basically, what he needed was a decent trim job, a change in his diet, and a little more exercise than he had been allowed. The owners went along with my suggestions, and when the offer was extended to be the "exclusive" hoofman for the ranch, I accepted. What became available to me was a huge experimental station where I could test my new "natural" trimming theories based on the wild horses I was still visiting.

Over the next four years, I did just that. And since none of the horses were shod (the Paso industry took a dim view of shoeing at the time), I could clearly see the results of my work without the detrimental effects of shoeing getting in the way. Almost immediately, the hooves began to respond to my "natural trim".[1] As time went by, we all began to notice that, where once there were hoof problems, now there were none. Preventively, the natural trim was a jewel, too. The attending vet, an elderly gentleman, marveled at the results and later wrote me to say that he had never seen so many sound horses in one place. I had to agree, because until then, I hadn't either!

---

[1] 2014 update: the term "natural trim" so common today had not yet been coined; but it was at this ranch that I first began to call it by that now popular name. This is to distinguish it from the farrier's "pasture trim" for barefoot turnout, the "flat trim" used by farriers for shoeing, and the many generic barefoot trims that have arisen opportunistically — and not without causing much harm to horses — in the wake of the natural trim based on the wild horse model.

The situation continued on for the next four years until the owners sold out and closed the ranch. But I had learned a lot in the meantime. First, that the wild horse model could be adapted to domestic hoof care. Second, that the natural trim had both preventive and healing value. And third, that naturally trimmed horses could also be ridden barefoot. The Peruvian trainers demonstrated the latter perfectly to my satisfaction. Even then I was aware that the dirt and pavement they rode over wouldn't even begin to challenge the hooves worn by our wild ones.

Still, I noticed also that even though my trims generated handsome hooves, they still didn't resemble the much tougher and quite elegant hooves one sees in the wild. Characteristically, wild hooves have extremely short toe walls, descended heel bulbs which endure ground contact passively, and relatively (by industry standards) high "angles-of-growth" (e.g., toe angle) even though the heels are comparatively short to non-existent when contrasted with domestic hooves. Eventually, I learned that these differences cannot be attributed to the hoof work, no matter how good it is, but to the lack of natural wear driven by the horse's instincts — in other words, behavior. (For a detailed discussion on the features of the wild horse foot, see my other written works.[1])

As time went by, I began to speculate that natural wear may only arise from natural behavior. such as we see in the wild — behavior that we seldom see among domestic horses. And to a lessor extent, from the effects of environment. I was pretty much stumped on this dilemma, when another opportunity presented itself that brought me closer to the vision for Paddock Paradise.

🐎

A 20,000 acre "horse rescue" ranch (1985)

Of the many visitors who came to the Paso ranch each year to purchase horses, was a young lady whose family owned and operated a huge cattle ranch in the coastal mountains further to the east. Of interest to me was that

---

[1]Go to my website (www.jaimejackson.com) for details, and also Star Ridge Publishing (www.star-ridge.com) to order copies of my, and others, works on the subject of natural hoof/horse care.

she also used the ranch as a "horse rescue" operation of sorts. She had acquired over 100 horses, and, as she explained the situation, they had free reign to go just about anywhere they wanted on the ranch. She had taken notice of my hoof work, and as she was aware that I used the wild horse model for the hooves, she was curious to know how naturally shaped the hooves were at her place. I agreed to go and check them out.

On my way to her ranch, I thought to myself, with a hundred horses roaming over a 30 square mile piece of property, surely there was ample space for the horses to move about on and generate naturally shaped hooves! Maybe even as nice as the wild horse hooves. The land at the ranch was arid and dry most of the year, so that was in their favor. Also, the owners fed hay, so the risks of grass founder were also reduced. And with that many horses, band/herd behavior was also within the realm of possibility to help matters. It seemed to me that everything was "lined up" perfectly for both natural boarding and naturally shaped hooves. I thought, the answer would lie here.

With much anticipation, I arrived at the ranch, where my hostess had brought in all the horses and secured them in a huge paddock. I entered and began to inspect the feet. Within minutes, if not sooner, the truth of the matter revealed itself. I turned to her and said, "I'm sorry, but these hooves aren't naturally shaped at all. In fact, they all need hoof work pretty bad." She couldn't believe it, and I was just as disappointed as she was. There wasn't much else to say, so I left as quickly as I had arrived.

The reader is welcome to try and figure this one out. At the time, I didn't know why the hooves were so unnaturally shaped given that there were so many "triggers" to make the whole thing work. I began to think that the horses just needed to move more. A lot more, perhaps. At the cattle ranch, the owner explained that the horses did group and move about the property, but that she didn't observe any patterns of movement or socialization that she hadn't seen on other horse properties. Most of the time, she related, they browsed about, mingled with the cattle now and then, and waited for hay to be thrown to them. They were never ridden either. In short, this pack had it made. By wild horse standards, they lived a lazy lifestyle and really didn't do much of anything. Well, that was a pretty good clue right there, and it reminded me of the Peruvian Pasos, who also more or less just milled around all day with nothing to do.

Finally came the experience that enabled me to "put it all together" and, not only paint a picture of Paddock Paradise in my mind, but to write my first book, *The Natural Horse*. Not surprisingly, it was our wild horses again who did it for me. But, not in the wild, rather amid rather unusual circumstances, and, admittedly, only by chance.

The BLM Wild Horse Corrals at Litchfield (1986)

During this period, I continued my visits not only to wild horse country, but to the BLM's Litchfield (CA), Burn's (OR) and Palomino Valley (NV) corrals where wild horses are processed following the gathers in the HMA's.[1] One day I happened to be at the Litchfield facility when

[1]Acronym for Herd Management Area. There are 186 active HMAs in eleven western states containing approximately 42,000 wild, free-roaming horses. See Lisa Dines, *the American Mustang Guidebook: History, Behavior, and State-by-State Directions on Where to Best View America's Wild Horses and How to Adopt and Gentle Your Very Own Mustang.* (Willow Creek Press: 2001) p.21.

BLM WRANGLERS
LITCHFIELD, CA (1986)
§
"As I stood watching the wild ones being processed at the BLM Corrals in N.E. Calif., I began to notice the large holding pastures immediately beyond the corrals seen here. The vision for Paddock Paradise was about to be borne . . ."

the outer pasture behind the roping corrals caught my eye.
I began to wonder what the wild horses were doing out
there, especially the ones just removed from their home
ranges hours before. These were horses very familiar with
life "on track". My curiosity struck, I took leave of the
heading and heeling and ventured to the fence line behind the office and barns where I could see what was
happening. What I found wasn't particularly earth-
shattering, but it was the missing piece to the puzzle I had
been waiting for.

Basically, hundreds of horses and burros were scattered
about in the huge pasture, which must have been three-
quarters of a mile deep and as wide. It just so happened
that it was feeding time too, and I could see a slow-moving
flatbed truck in the distance with several hired hands
pushing off square bales to the horses who were more or
less trailing behind in small groups. As the hay hit the
ground, one group of horses stopped to feed. Further along,
another group claimed its bale, and so forth until all the

BURROS LINE UP FOR INTERNMENT
§
The ground in the outer paddock was as rugged and abrasive as in their home range where hours before they roamed in complete freedom.

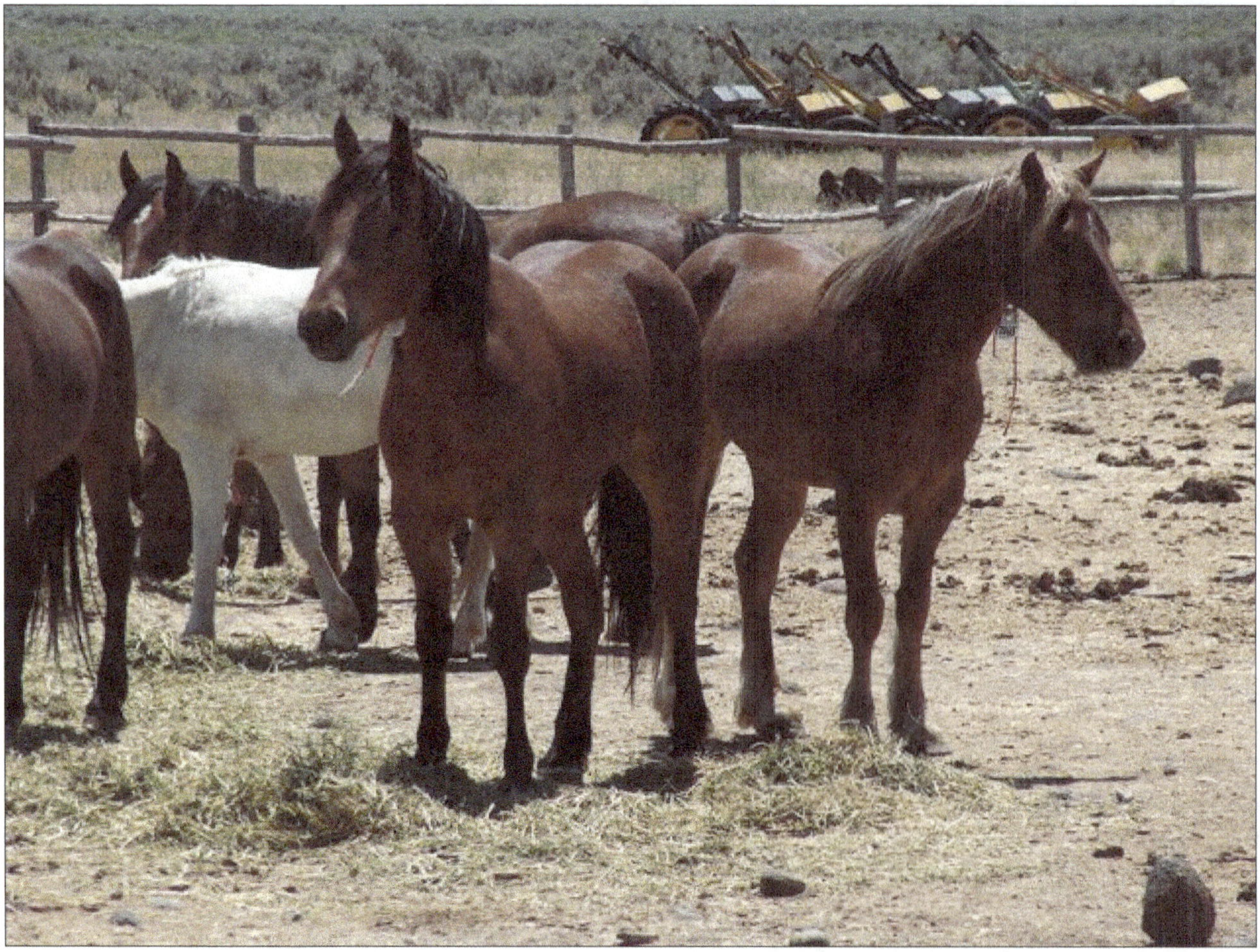

horses, spread all over the field, were busy munching on whatever hay the government was feeding at the time. Under these circumstances, there was enough competition among horses, that to get one's share and fill, everyone had better stay put and eat. Apparently, this feeding scenario occurred twice a day. In between, the horses more or less stood there and did nothing. And it was clear too that they really had nothing to do. The latter was reflected in their shabby hooves (*facing page*), which, after several weeks or so of this compounded idleness, had began to deteriorate from their exemplary form seen in the home range.

Now bear in mind that just hours before a group of horses is introduced to this rather traditional paddock network, they had been living lives of constant movement in the home range. Yet, as soon as they arrive in the outer pasture behind the corrals, whatever allegiances they had to the old way are abandoned. The first notable difference was that almost immediately upon being released from the processing corrals, they began to disperse and, through relative dominance, became absorbed into existing hierarchies among the horses already present. Track behavior, as we know it in the wild, no longer occurs, and movement becomes relatively stationary and, notwithstanding competition for feed and defending one's sphere of intolerance, unmotivated.

WILD HORSES AT LITCHFIELD, CA (2005)
§
What is a fence in the mind of a horse?

I began to look for clues. Could it be the mere presence of the perimeter fencing? Might the horse be thinking, "Ah, there's the fence, and so there's no point trying to do anything. Let's just give up and stand around and do nothing." But there are fences everywhere in wild horse country, and I came to realize that in the horse's mind, a fence is simply an obstacle — not a death knell for natural movement. Arguably their cognitive awareness doesn't even interpret the integral parts of a fence like we humans do. Invariably, they learn these things the hard way.

Let's say, by way of example, that you own six horses, and keep them all in a fenced paddock. Somehow or another, five "escape" and one gets left behind:

Among the escapees is your "alpha" mare, who temporarily keeps the "herd" close to the paddock. The loner is anxious about this, and nervously paces the fence line wishing he were with the others. Now the alpha mare decides to head down the lane to visit your neighbor's herd. The loner becomes hysterical, and we see that he may even decide to jump the fence — a dangerous move as he might become ensnared in the barbed wire or whatever the fence is comprised of. Now we cut open the fence line for him to make his escape, and announce the fact to him. But, we notice that he cannot even perceive the gate no matter how much we yell the fact to him or point to it. His cognitive mind cannot compute the information or the reality. Not until he paces the fence line far enough to where he actually stumbles upon the opening will he recognize it — and make his escape to join the others. But once he does, he will never forget it! Put him or any horse in the same situation and whether a second, minute, day, month or year later, he will immediately run to that spot in the fence line, regardless if the gate is still there or not, to try and get out. It may be a fence with a gate to us, but in the equine mind, it is only an obstacle with an opening to get through. Humans and horses process information differently.

And on this point hinges the entire premise of Paddock

Paradise: our challenge is to create a living space that suits the equine mind, and not ours. More specifically, one that *triggers* in the horse natural behavioral responses to his environment. I believe the problem with most equine confinement systems today is that they either outright obstruct such responses, or reward the horse to disengage from them. Either way, the horse fails to behave naturally, and a plethora of problems, from the mind to the foot, then erupt.

Both the 20,000 acre horse rescue and Litchfield taught me that horses, like many people, will simply adapt to whatever is available to them The horse readily adapts to the new food delivery system and the old ways are abandoned. When the stimulus to band and move together naturally is removed or denied, the underlying instinct becomes dormant. Asleep. How do we create a situation which will bring these instincts and natural behaviors back into play?

Many horse owners want their horses to live natural lives, but are frustrated in their attempts to get them to cooperate. I've been told, as an example, "I place hay all around their paddock to get them to move from one pile to the next, but they'll only eat certain piles. If I put gravel or other rock around their hay to get them to toughen their hooves, they'll walk around the rocks or refuse to eat altogether. I feel so guilty and I'm afraid they'll starve, so I have to put out new piles of hay so they will eat." Or, "No matter how much space I give them, or food to eat, they still stand around most of the day, doing nothing. What else can I do?"

The "trick" of course is figuring out how to do it. To "convince" domestic horses that they are capable of behaving naturally like their healthy wild cousins. The beauty of the Paddock Paradise model is that, through a unique fencing configuration — adaptable to most if not all equine properties — and strategically applied stimuli, it "tricks" the horse into thinking he's in wild horse country, "paradise" in other words. Instead of resisting natural movement, he willingly engages in it. Through stimulated natural movement, he becomes healthier, and this is our major goal. By way of comparison, marine biologists have learned that by putting captive sharks in aquariums with "currents", they will instinctively move against the current and remain healthy and behave like sharks in the wild. But remove the current, and they become somewhat disoriented, and behave unnaturally and are prone to becoming sick.

Some advocates believe that "environment" is the overriding factor in achieving success. But the domestic horses in the 20,000 acre horse rescue operation, or in domestic confinement systems with a plethora of natural features, still fail to move naturally and defy their owners' efforts to "get them going". Once more, I profess that it is behavior and environment working together, that lies at the bottom of all natural movement and truly naturally shaped hooves.

This then, brings us to the final chapter of *Paddock Paradise*. To me, this is the fun part of natural horse care. But there are ground rules we need to acknowledge and abide by, if it is to work for us. These, not surprisingly, are the "lessons from the wild" discussed in Chapter 1. And the time to apply them has arrived.

Lessons from the Wild Applied

The beauty of Paddock Paradise is that it applies (within reasonable limits) to virtually all kinds of terrains and climates. The size, shape and location of the property you keep your horse on is less important than how you use it. In the U.S., as with most places on the planet, property is divided legally along meridian (longitude and latitude) lines. So most of us are dealing with rectangular shaped properties to start. This is okay. Horses don't really recognize or even care what size or shape the property is they're living on. The only thing that matters to them is that their basic needs (mainly food and socialization) are being met.

The "lessons from the wild" described in Chapter 1 provide us with the essential guidelines for constructing Paddock Paradise. These are summarized in the chart at right. If we violate these lessons too much, we will be stuck with expensive hoof care and vet bills. So, to keep him moving and moving naturally (the "key"), the lessons must be applied diligently and consistently. Look at it this way, the more faithfully we apply the lessons, the less work for us, the more money we will save, and the healthier our horses are going to be.

Your property: any size, any shape.

First, you don't need a large property for Paddock Paradise. Several acres will do. You don't need land the size of a typical home range (like the 20,000 acre ranch). In fact, the larger your property is, proportionally the less of it you will need to use! Again, it's how we use the land, not how much we own. Paddock Paradise uses only a fraction of our available land. In effect, it takes our land back from the horse and returns it to us for other possible uses. More on that later.

Your property can be just about any type: mountain, valley, high desert, low desert, meadow, forest, beach, To the horse, it makes no difference. He is perfectly capable of

*On track in
Paddock Paradise*

—

*AANHCP
Field Headquarters
Lompoc, CA, USA*

Your Property

—

*Any size,
any shape*

"Lessons from the Wild" for
Natural Equine Behavior and Movement

Lesson	*Description*	*Type*
Agonistic	Alert, alarm, and flight; aggression; stallion interactions; influence of rank order on daily activity.	Extraordinary
Comfort	Self-indulgent (sunning, shelter-seeking, licking, nibbling, scratching, rubbing, rolling, shaking and skin twitching, tail switching); mutual interactions (mutual grooming and symbiotic relationship with birds).	Ordinary
Communicative	Visual expressions, acoustical expressions, squeal, nickers, whinny, groan, blow, snort, snore, other sounds, tactile interactions, chemical exchanges.	Extraordinary Ordinary
Coprophagous	Consumption of dung.	Unusual
Dominance	Pecking order and alliances.	Extraordinary
Eliminative	Urinating and defecating.	Ordinary
Ingestive	Feeding, drinking, nursing.	Ordinary
Investigative	Curiosity.	Extraordinary Ordinary
Ontogeny	Perinatal and postnatal.	Extraordinary Ordinary
Play	Solitary, foal-mother, sibling, younger-older.	Extraordinary
Reproductive	Sexual (male), sexual (female), and maternal.	Extraordinary Ordinary
Resting	Standing and recumbency.	Ordinary
Sleep	Recumbency.	Ordinary
Social Group	Herd and band structure, migratory, roles.	Extraordinary Ordinary
Social Pair Bonding	Mare-foal, foal-mare, peer, heterosexual, paternal, interspecies.	Extraordinary Ordinary
Territorial	Home range and territoriality (stud piles).	Ordinary

adapting to most any environment or climate. Paddock Paradise will take advantage of this leeway he provides us.

Paddock Paradise also ignores the shape of your property, which can be any shape (or size). In fact, the final design of your Paddock Paradise will be up to you and you can adapt it to all or part of your property. In the next chapter I will show you an example created by horse owners who simply used their imaginations. In a moment, though, I will start you off with a basic pattern (template) from which you can adapt your own unique design.

It is my personal hope that owners of horse boarding facilities will use Paddock Paradise as a means of getting horses out of stalls, conventional paddocks, and other modes of close confinement that simulate "predator" environments that are so harmful to the mental and physical well-being of horses.

Getting Started "On Track"

We have several objectives to start. First, we want to simulate the wild horse's natural home range, replete with a "track" like we learned about in Chapter 2. Second, we want to provide him with lots of things to do along the way, activities which stimulate natural movement while he is on track.

Getting Started

The track and vital stimulation.

It's important that we keep our horses moving "on track" because that is the natural way for their species. On the 20,000 acre ranch and at Litchfield, we find the horses all "dispersing"; living life in sedentary groups "off track", in other words. The horse needs stimulation to "move forward" on track, taking breaks along the way to keep his interest while satisfying his natural need for routine, In Paddock Paradise this is easy enough to do because we are going to literally confine him to his "track" (with a few diversions spaced here and there), in effect preventing him from dispersing. Activities along the way will provide the necessary stimuli to motivate him to move along forward on track.

The "95–5 Principle"

Over the years I have listened to many arguments against natural boarding (i.e., why it can't work), one being that it is unrealistic, if not impossible, to get horses to move vigorously and sufficiently enough to do them (and their hooves) any good. Commonly: "I would have to ride my horse 30 miles a day to get him and his hooves looking natural. And who has time to do that?" I'm not sure how this purported "lesson from the wild" managed to take hold in the minds of so many horse owners, but the premise is fallacious and riding one's horse that much every day is actually unnecessary and probably harmful. Besides, who has time to do that anyway?

In fact, while wild horses may move that distance (usually less) in a given day, the majority of the time or "distance traveled" is spent walking, eating, and resting. In other words, horses spent most of their daily time engaging in "ordinary" behaviors (see "Lessons From The Wild" chart, p. 67) while on track. Riding, due to the fact that the horse is carrying the weight of a human, constitutes "extraordinary" behavior. While more definitive research on the subject of band behavior is badly needed to give clarity here, it was my observation in wild horse country that movement based on ordinary behavior constituted about 95 percent of their locomotive energy expended; extraordinary behavior only 5 percent, or less. This ratio of ordinary-to-extraordinary behavior is what I call the 95–5 Principle.

The 95–5 Principle helps us to interpret the relationship of the various behaviors which may take place within, and outside of, Paddock Paradise. Due to the nature of the track's construction, which favors ordinary behavior, I recommend that all extraordinary behavior take place outside Paddock Paradise. How this works exactly is easier to explain later after we've put the track together.

The good news here, according to the 95–5 Principle, is that, your horse only has to walk, eat, and sleep most of the time (his 95 percent quota) to develop a healthy body and beautiful naturally shaped hooves! A mere fraction of the time (his 5 percent quota) is spent engaging in vigorous behavior (movement), and at that, you don't really need to

95-5 Principle

—

Ordinary and extraordinary Behaviors.

be riding him, because he can do it on his own with his equine buddies. No daily 30 mile rides needed here! This is not to suggest, however, that the 5 percent quota is unimportant, only that a relatively small period of time of vigorous (and natural) movement is required to build healthy bodies and strong, naturally shaped hooves.

Humans not allowed

—

Our place in Paddock Paradise.

No Humans Allowed

Paddock Paradise is the horse's home, or more precisely, his *home range*. I believe we should respect it as such, and, for the most part, stay out of it. This is the way wild horses prefer it in their home land, and what is natural for them should apply equally, or nearly so, to his domestic cousin. After all, your horse doesn't intrude into your home, does he?

There are actually other important reasons for the "no humans allowed" clause of Paddock Paradise. Foremost, we are trying to simulate a wild equine environment in which he can prosper. Turning his world into a human playground (I was once asked if the track could be used as a jumping concourse!) only serves to undermine our objective. Within Paddock Paradise, we strive to create natural conditions for the horse. That which we create are carefully calculated to elicit behavioral responses, which, in turn, catalyze natural movement on track. Accordingly, we should make every effort to minimize our many human influences, while facilitating the scents, sounds and socialization patterns of the wild equine lifestyle.

The track

—

Central artery of Paddock Paradise.

Creating the Track

The "track" is the central "artery" of Paddock Paradise. It is the main passageway along which we seek to propel the horse forward naturally. Putting the horse "on track", thus, is our main concern. In the wild, the track weaves its way through the home range, the horse "glued" to and motivated forward upon it by his many survival instincts. Indeed, the horse's will to survive keeps him habitually on track, for he craves order and familiarity as he negotiates his environment to find the things he needs to live. Anything which threatens to jar him off his course or deprive him of his natural resources, therefore, is perceived by the horse as a direct threat to his survival. The wild horse therefore naturally resists any intrusion or depletion of the home range that forces him off track. In short, he will cling to the track that meets his needs with the same unrelenting tenacity and force that holds metal filings to a magnet. In the words of Aristotle, it is his *telos* — his Way — and he cannot help himself before it. Paddock Paradise recognizes and serves his teleology by putting him "on track" and sustaining him there for his own good.

Let us construct a basic template for Paddock Paradise, starting with a frame of reference most horse owners can identify with. The typical horse pasture, paddock, or stall is generally rectangular in shape:

§
Rectangular con-figuration typical of most horse pastures, pad-docks, and stalls.

Assuming that the reader no longer accepts close confinement as a humane system for boarding horses, we can dismiss the stall and conventional small holding paddocks from this discussion. I would encourage owners of private or public boarding facilities using stall and paddock networks not to panic but to consider the merits of what we are trying to accomplish here, since the surrounding grounds of most operations readily transpose to facilitate the architecture and track dynamics of Paddock Paradise.

Now I ask the reader to imagine any suitable equine property beyond one acre in size — once more, the actual size or shape of the land is irrelevant. Let's say, for discussion, that you own 5 acres and 6 horses. For effect, let's also say that the five acres has a sturdy perimeter fence, and is planted in a combination of woods and lush green

grasses, the latter known to cause life-threatening laminitis — one of the deadliest killers and lamers of horses
known today. In other words, by filling in the previous
diagram a bit, we have something like this:

Obviously, we can't leave our horses stranded in there
with this kind of threat! Ah, but we can, and this is where
Paddock Paradise comes in. The first thing we want to do
is create a second fence line *inside* the perimeter fence.
This will be an electric fence, and we will place it approximately 10 to 15 feet away from the perimeter fence.
Now, the horses are contained within two fences: a sturdy,
stationary perimeter fence and an inner adjustable electric fence:

Creating "the track"

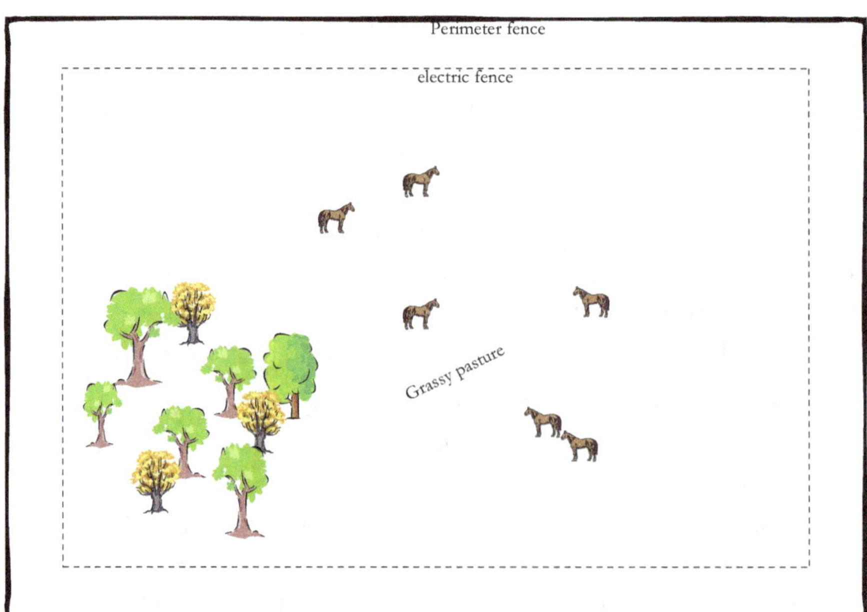

It doesn't take long for the horses to learn to stay clear of the electric fence either. The electric fence will soon play an important role in Paddock Paradise. Okay, we are now ready to place the horses inside Paddock Paradise, and "on track". And it's as simple as this:

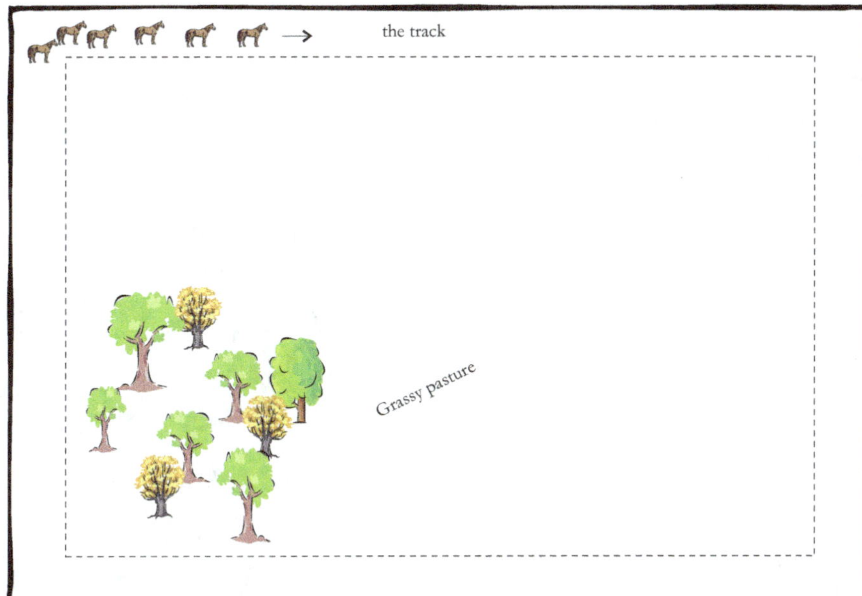

Diagrammatic of horses on track in Paddock Paradise

§

Horses on track at AANHCP Field Headquarters, Lompoc, CA

Jill Willis

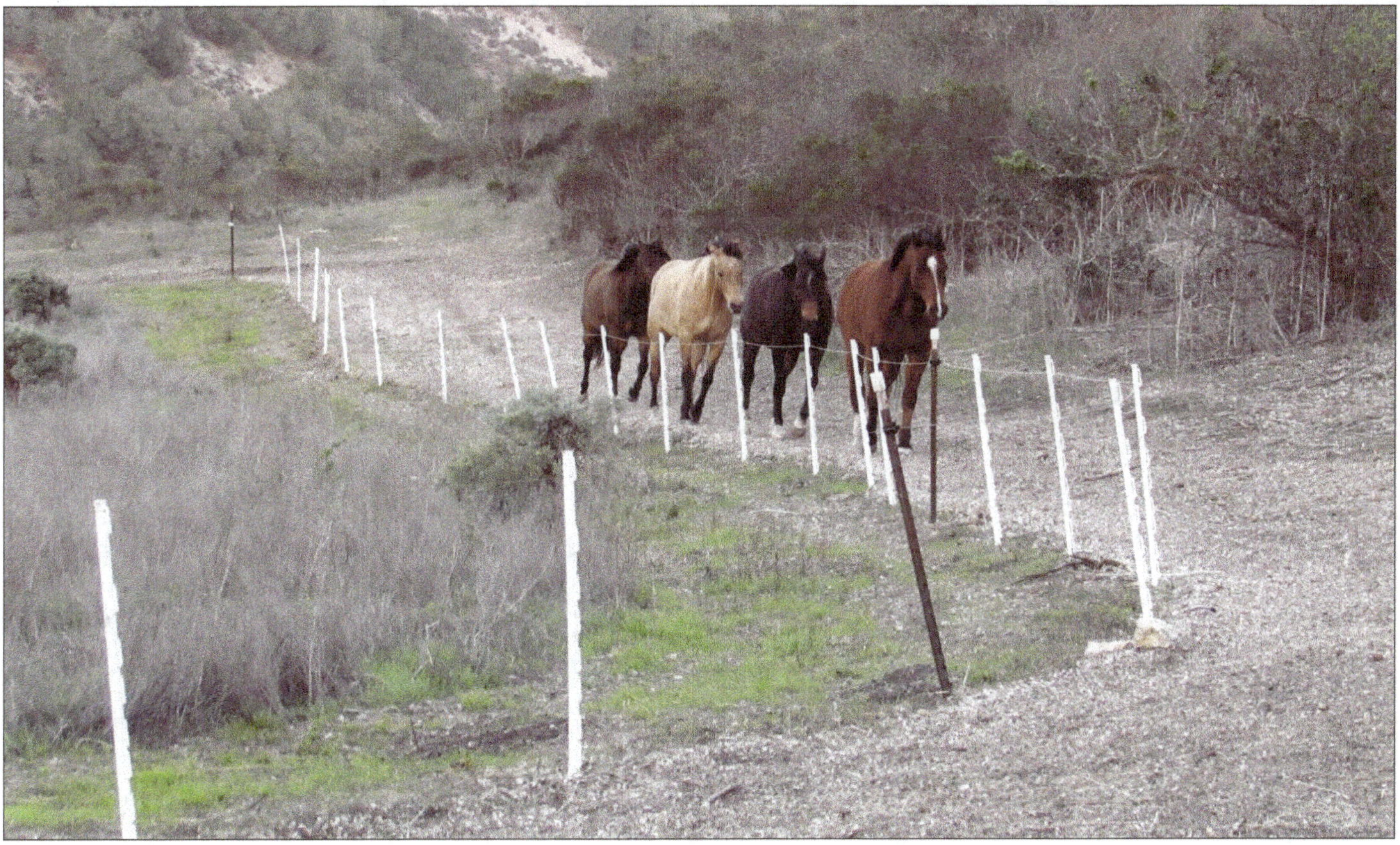

Although we've not even begun to flesh out the many possible features of Paddock Paradise, early experiments reveal that horses begin to move almost immediately on track, and usually clockwise! The impetus to move thusly is probably instigated by the animal's innate curiosity towards his environment. "What is this?" is probably running through his equine mind. And the solution is obvious to him too — simple movement to go check it out. We capitalize on this group curiosity (no one wants to be left behind in wild horse country or Paddock Paradise!) by building in specific *stimuli* that will tend to keep the horses going forward naturally as a band, or as a grouping of bands,

This is where the "lessons from the wild" come in. Indeed, if we as humans view the track as the main "artery" of Paddock Paradise, then the many "lessons" along its path will constitute its vital nervous system. Holistically speaking, the lessons are those behavioral motivations that fire the horse's instincts, causing him to move and live as though he were in the wild. Life in Paddock Paradise, while perhaps peculiar to our human way of thinking about how horses should live, will, if we are faithful in carrying out its basic principles, present a contrast to the dull, harmful and "lifeless" world of conventional confinement systems that suppress natural movement. And the vision promises a healthier animal in our midst.

Okay, it's time to add those lessons onto our track. In reality, I recommend that horse owners do this systematically, by creating a track with

Holistically speaking, the lessons are those behavioral motivations that fire the horse's instincts, causing him to move and live as though he were in the wild.

stimuli that correspond to the natural behaviors listed in the chart posted at the beginning of this chapter. The discussion that follows provides general guidelines for doing this, and these you should be able to adapt readily to your specific plot of land, regardless of its size or shape.

On the next page (*overleaf*) is a "master template" that corresponds to the discussion. I've added numbers that cross-link the discussion to the diagram. You'll want to refer often to it, but bear in mind that you will probably create a different look and track than what you see here. Chapter 4 gives an example of a "real life" paddock, which incorporates only a fraction of the possibilities recommended here (the owners did not have the benefit of this book when they created it), yet the horses are doing very well on track, and their owners are delighted.

On this note, let's start creating our track beginning with diet, since food, along with curiosity, are going to be foremost on our horses' minds.

Diet and Feeding Behavior

The first regimen of stimuli should relate directly to the horse's most pressing survival need, one nearly always present in his mind due to the nature of his digestive tract: diet. While research of the wild horse diet and feeding behavior is still forthcoming, there are basics we can apply to Paddock Paradise with good results.

It may come as a surprise to many horse owners, but horses naturally spend most of their time not resting, but eating — and eating on the move, seldom stationary in one place as is common with too many domestic horses unnaturally confined. Studies of wild horses I've cited earlier, corroborate my own observations that horses spend over half their daily lives feeding. And that figure increases during the winter, due to the diminished availability of forage on many winter

A monarch stallion surveys his kingdom . . .

rangelands.[1] Feeding behavior peaks in the early morning and late evening, reaching a low mid-day.

Foremost, we should recognize that horses (like cattle) are natural browsers, that is, "nibblers" who eat a little of this and that as they move along. This is in contrast to "grazing in place" behavior, typical of domestic pastures wherein horses eat everything they can fit into their stomachs, especially green grass, with as little movement as possible! But this is not natural feeding behavior for the equine species. The horse must be encouraged to nibble *and* move. We help by the placement of feed on track and the quantities provided,

My research of the wild horse diet suggests that horses will benefit from being fed a mix of grass-type hays, unsweetened oats in small quantities, mineral and salt licks, and water. Until we learn more about the horse's natural diet, I would caution horse owners from feeding much of anything else, particularly horses suffering or recovering from laminitis.[2]

[1] C.B. Marlow, et al. See winter feeding distribution graph below.

[2] See my dietary recommendations in, *Laminitis: A Plague*. Unfortunately, the veterinary, university, and feed industry sectors are sound asleep on researching the wild horse diet, even though it sustains tens of thousands of healthy horses in the U.S. Great Basin. Given the natural diet's supreme importance, the AANHCP will continue to lobby for such investigation.

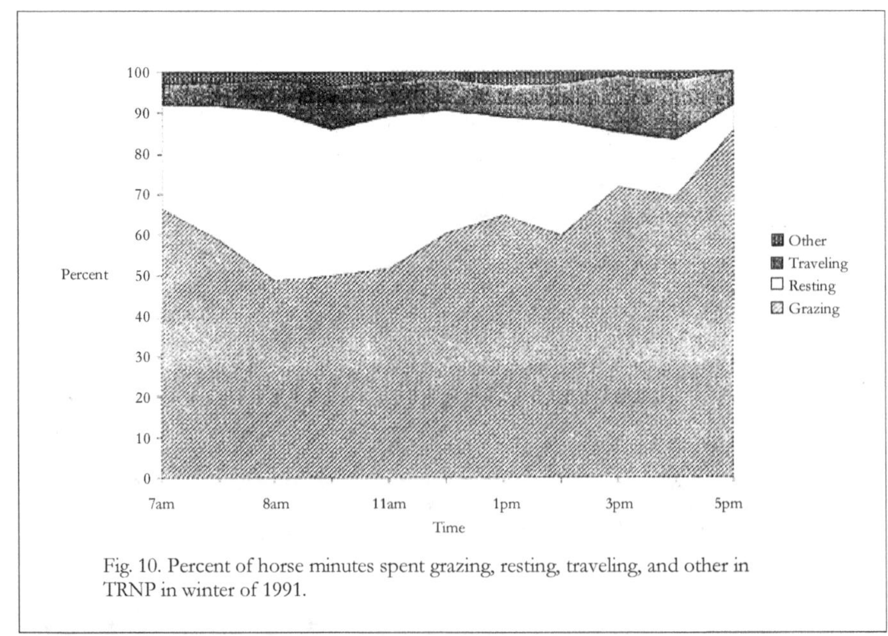

Fig. 10. Percent of horse minutes spent grazing, resting, traveling, and other in TRNP in winter of 1991.

Customarily, horses are thrown whatever amount of hay, grain, supplements, and so forth, we think they will need for the day, usually in one, or at most, two feedings a day. The horse is left to stand right there and eat what he can. Depending on how much and what is provided, as well as competition pressure from other horses, he may eat it all at once or take a break (but to do what?) now and then. This won't work in Paddock Paradise, and, fortunately, the construction of the track makes it easy to feed a much better and more natural way.

What we want to do is spread the feed, particularly the hay, around the track at regulated intervals. [Time to go to the "Paddock Paradise Template", see *Overleaf*, #1]. The idea is to space the hay so that the horses will keep moving. If we place too much in one spot, or in only one location, we will encourage "camping". Camping (discussed later) is okay, but it shouldn't be feeding behavior based. I would liken this to the opportunistic "greener pastures" syndrome. Once introduced, our horses, either from curiosity or hunger, will begin to explore the entire track. As each new hay "nugget" is discovered, they will quite readily want to move to the next, and before they finish what they've started. Indeed, competition for forage from fellow band members will help drive this syndrome. So, the pressure is on everyone to get going to eat. And it's good for them. The alternative, gluttony — eating "super-sized" meals in one place — is, to my thinking, a prescription for indolence and colic.

Of course, it is nearly impossible for me to figure the spacing for you, because it will depend on the number of horses on track, how much you decide to throw per pile, how many piles you decide to throw, and the size of the track itself.

You may be asking yourself, how much hay should I put out? There should be enough hay placed so that the horses will never finish what is given to them in a day's time, or whatever time interval you decide to feed by. As mentioned earlier, I also recommend feeding a variety of hays — not just one. Who wants to eat just one thing? And who can survive eating just one thing?

So, scanning the entire track (PP Template), you will

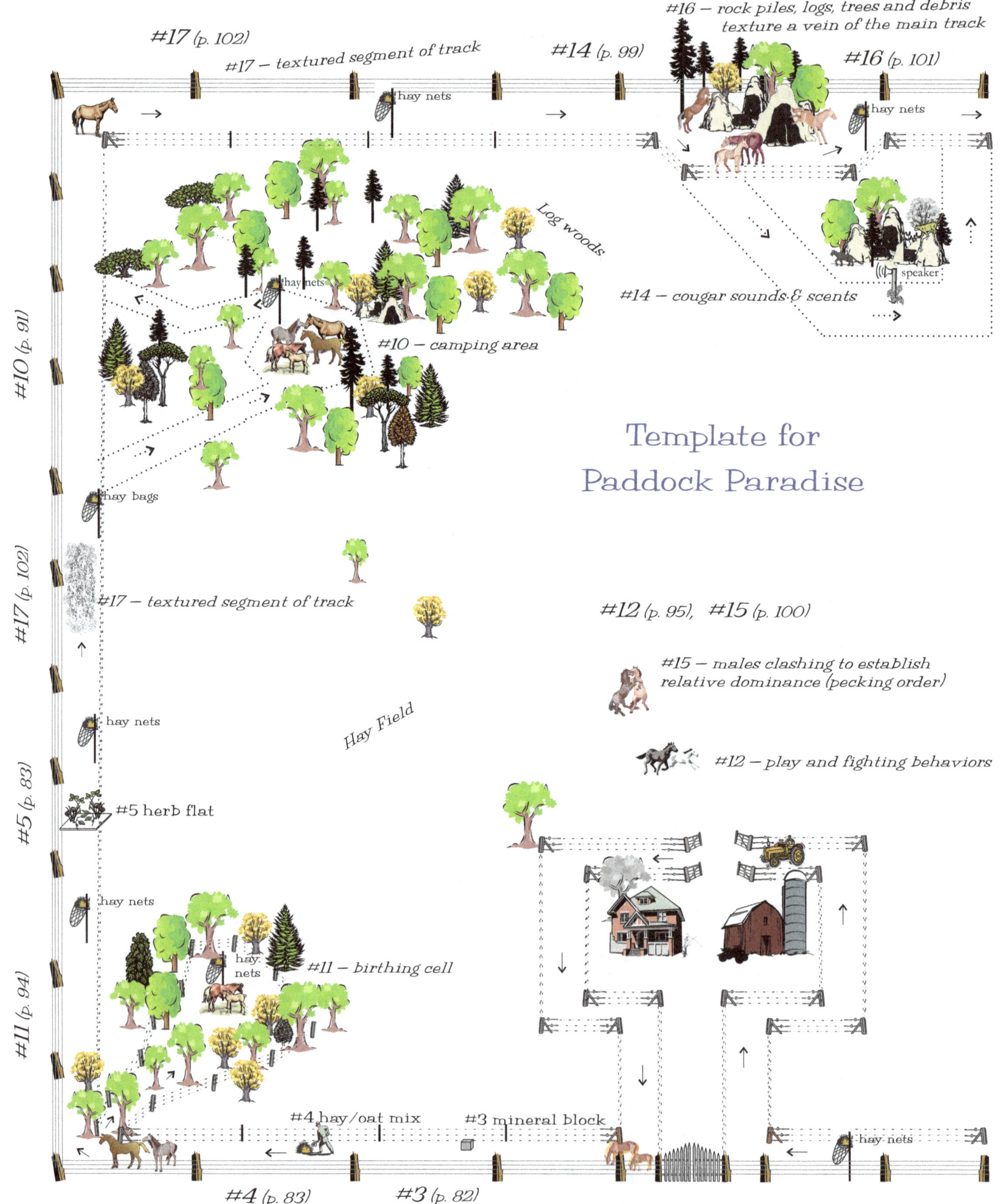
#17 (p. 102)
#17 — textured segment of track
#14 (p. 99)
#16 — rock piles, logs, trees and debris texture a vein of the main track
#16 (p. 101)
hay nets
hay nets
Log woods
hay nets
speaker
#14 — cougar sounds & scents
#10 — camping area
Template for Paddock Paradise
#10 (p. 91)
hay bags
#17 (p. 102)
#17 — textured segment of track
#12 (p. 95), #15 (p. 100)
#15 — males clashing to establish relative dominance (pecking order)
hay nets
Hay Field
#12 — play and fighting behaviors
#5 (p. 83)
#5 herb flat
hay nets
hay nets
#11 — birthing cell
#11 (p. 94)
#4 hay/oat mix
#3 mineral block
hay nets
#4 (p. 83)
#3 (p. 82)

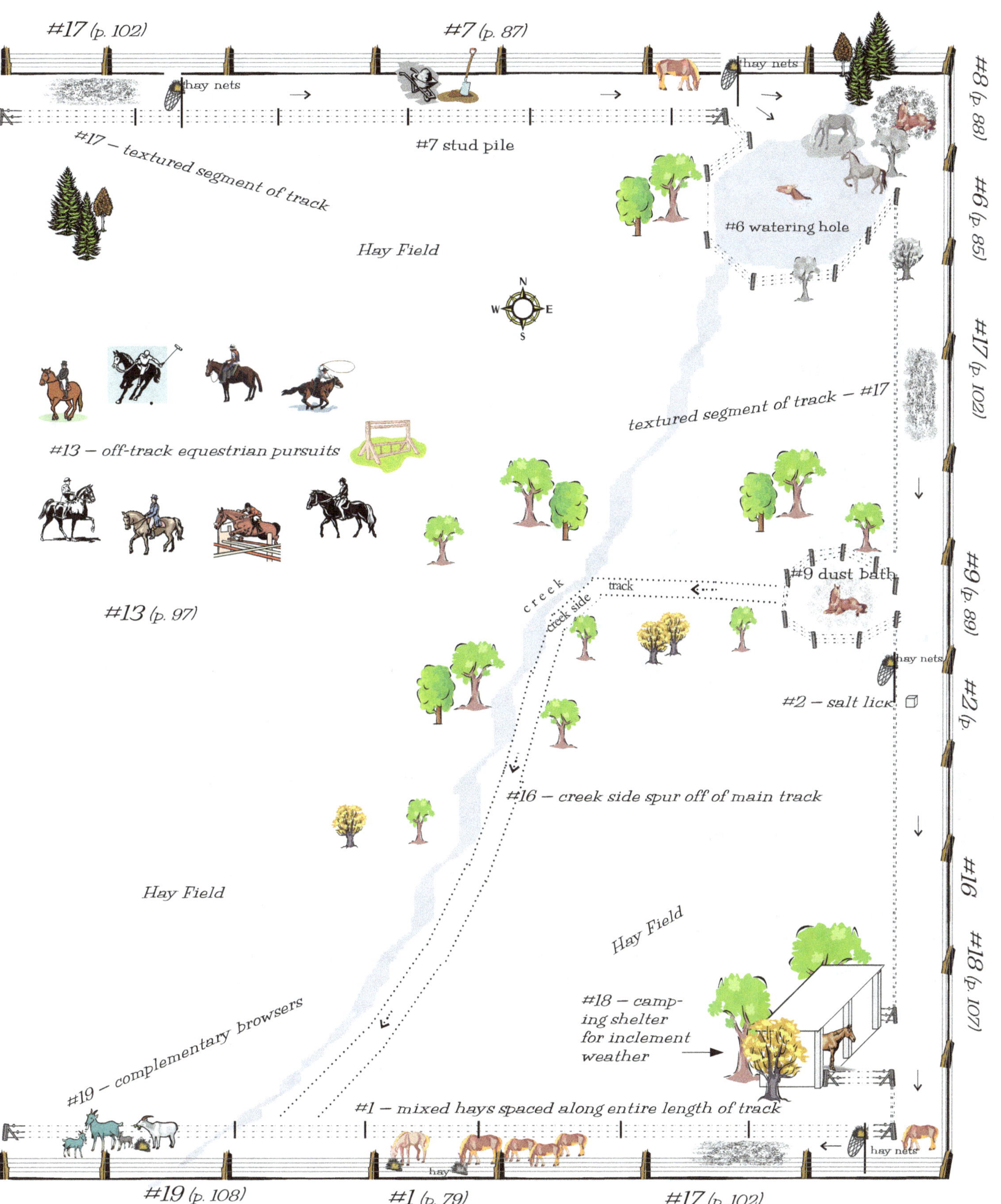

#17 (p. 102)
#7 (p. 87)
#8 (p. 88)
hay nets
hay nets
#17 — textured segment of track
#7 stud pile
#6 (p. 85)
#6 watering hole
Hay Field
N
W E
S
#17 (p. 102)
textured segment of track — #17
#13 — off-track equestrian pursuits
#9 dust bath
#13 (p. 97)
#9 (p. 89)
creek
creek side
track
hay nets
#2 — salt lick
#2 (p.
#16 — creek side spur off of main track
Hay Field
#16
Hay Field
#18 — camping shelter for inclement weather
#18 (p. 107)
#19 — complementary browsers
#1 — mixed hays spaced along entire length of track
hay
hay nets
#19 (p. 108)
#1 (p. 79)
#17 (p. 102)

now see that we have our hay positioned along the track at time-configured space intervals. We can also set out salt [#2. PP Template] and minerals blocks [#3, PP Template] along the way, perhaps several of each, spaced strategically around the track. Calcium too, I have observed personally and reported in Chapter 1, seems to play an important part in the wild horse diet, as the horses will actually dig deposits out of the ground with their hooves, grind it up into a powder with their teeth, and then swallow it. Calcium so consumed may play a role in cancer prevention in wild horse herds, as well as satisfy other nutritional needs. Because of the grinding action, it may also be how they unwittingly keep their teeth so healthy and free of sharp edges — there are no vets out there to rasp the dental arcades. This is another area of vital research that is being neglected by our scientific community.

I recommend that you consider breaking up the salt, mineral, and calcium blocks into large chunks and burying them in concentrations along the track just below or at the surface of the ground. The idea here is to encourage pawing behavior — to stimulate the horse to dig it out of the ground with his hooves. We want the hooves to work as much as possible in Paddock Paradise. "Mining" the earth for vital nutrients is part of the horse's telos, and we must strive to find clever ways to make him "work for his living".

Oats (unsweetened whole, crimped, or steamed) seem to be a safe addition to the horse's diet,, mouthfuls at a time being better than bucketfuls. Better yet, I recommend mixing it with the hay [#4, PP Template], rather than feeding it free choice. Mouthfuls upon mouthfuls of straight grain, any grain, are probably an invitation to digestive disorder — including the deadly duo of colic and laminitis. There is some discussion among my colleagues in the natural care movement of "gluing" oats to hay in a harmless way. The idea is to balance the oats with the dry grass, as we would see in the wild. You might try sprin-

#2, #3

—

PP Template

We frequently see our horses at the AANHCP Paddock Paradise licking and/or biting at various rocks. Safe to assume they know what they are doing and why they are doing it. So much research that has yet to be conducted on the Great Basin horses could provide us with a wealth of information about keeping our horses healthy. This is seven year old Chance on July 11, 2013.

kling the oats in the hay and see what happens.

Natural care advocates predict that special "feeding flats" comprised of herbs, certain legumes, and other natural substances providing micro-nutrients for the horse's diet could be manufactured by the feed industry. Or by industrious horse owners with green thumbs who wish to plant the edges of the track with the same things. The flats (or planted herbs) would be set out like the hay/grain piles at intervals on the track and secured firmly to the ground [#5, PP Template]. The idea here is to facilitate browsing behavior whereby the horse uses his prehensile lips and teeth to "pluck" the herbs from the flats (or ground). This tugging and incising action simulates natural browsing behavior more so than munching "loose hay" does, which requires very little plucking, albeit much important masticating with the molars. Such browsing action, nevertheless, strengthens and wears the teeth naturally and should be encouraged in Paddock Paradise.

#5
—
PP Template

At the AANHCP Field Headquarters and Paddock Para-

dise, hay is fed using hay nets hung from poles, like this:. Hays nets are clustered in "feed stations" spaced along the track, where there is one hay net per horse. Hay nets so slung from poles are ideal for many reasons. For example, the small openings force the horse to pluck and nibble rather than "wolf" down their hay; as they eat the hay, the bad lowers towards the ground, so they also eat at a range of heights — like we see in the wild; they do not soil their hay with urine or feces; the wind does not blow hay away; rain drains through the nets and when hay is properly rationed, mold is not an issue; nets can be stuffed at the barn at any time and taken to the feed stations at any time, thereby accommodating the owner's busy schedule.

Recalling the 95-5 Principle, stimulating ample amounts of natural feeding behavior is an important part of meeting the 95 percent movement (ordinary behavior) quota. This should become easier to do as research elucidating the wild horse diet and feeding behavior provides us with new information on what, how much, when, and where to feed horses in Paddock Paradise.

Water and Watering Behavior

Closely related to diet and feeding behavior is the need for water and natural watering behavior in Paddock Paradise. Natural care advocates believe strongly that the health of the horse and his feet is greatly enhanced by his freedom to enter water as described below. The obvious need of the horse to quench his thirst is another stimulus to cause movement on track. As with his hay, grain, and mineral/salt blocks we want to provide water at ground level.. There are various ways to accomplish this, but probably the most natural way is for the horse to stand in the water he is drinking. In fact, going one step further, consider creating a watering "hole" large enough for your horses to wade and bathe in. In the wild, horses take great delight in bathing and pawing the water during the warm summer months. In winter, they only enter the holes to drink — even cracking ice over water holes to access the water.

In the wild, bathing behavior is normally followed by rolling behavior along the sandy banks of many water holes. These "mud" baths evidently aid in the health of the horse's coat, while affording natural protection from biting insects. Hoof-to-water (mud) contact is also important to the health and conditioning of the horse's feet. The effect of the water is to cleanse the commissures of the frog in the volar dome, while the moist mud slightly softens the outer keritinized protein which cements the hoof (capsule) together. Pitted immediately against the dry, firm ground of the track, the hoof is further molded and honed under the immense compressional forces driven by natural behavior, Any loose or frayed tubular strands, unchecked bars, or unworn flaps of frog are almost instantaneously planished into a smooth, rock hard epidermal crust necessary for any horse's foot to take the beating that comes with everyday life on the track. We can simulate this strategic defense mechanism of the hoof by carefully orchestrating watering behavior in Paddock Paradise.

Paddock Paradise, shows a water hole at left and track at right leading past it.

Practically speaking, one can either incorporate existing streams or ponds in Paddock Paradise, or create one from scratch [#6, PP Template]. Here's a suggestion: Either by hand, or with a small tractor, dig out a corner of Paddock Paradise to the depth of one to three feet (at the deep end), and wide enough to hold several horses (in the wild, they learn to take turns based on relative dominance). Line the "water hole" with one of the new "bullet proof" tarps available from drip irrigation suppliers, or some other water impervious material if your ground "leaks" profusely. Set a spigot or drip line to the water hole, letting the water flow just enough to keep it full and the edges muddy.

#6

—

PP Template

The horses will, sooner or later, depending largely on temperature, feel their way further and further into the water hole, drinking first, bathing later as their confidence and curiosity, and the urge to engage their native behaviors, all take hold. They may urinate or defecate in it. This is okay, and make no effort to "clean" or disinfect the water hole. It is a myth that horses must drink "clear, clean" water to be healthy. Our (wild horse) model proves precisely the opposite to be true. Here, I am not talking about the imbibing of carcinogenic and other man-made toxic chemicals (pesticides, fertilizers, and even Chlorine and Fluoride mixed with "city" water), but the consumption of naturally biodegraded matter derived from living things that would be found in and around watering holes utilized by wild horses. Arguably, the consumption of bacteria derived from naturalized watering holes may contribute to the strengthening of the horse's immune system.

As in wild horse country, our water hole should additionally be rounded out with an adjacent sandy, or better, loamy area — I will take this up shortly in another section. Again the purpose here is to encourage rolling behavior which conditions and protects the horse's coat.

So, with a little clever imagination, we are able to expand our Paddock Paradise to include a natural watering hole for drinking, bathing and rolling purposes.

Dung, Copraphagous & Dominance Behaviors (Ordinary)

Since our horses will be living "on track" for the majority of their lives, the accumulation of dung will sooner or later become an issue, at least in smaller paddocks. While the majority of dung can be removed as necessary, our model shows us that a certain amount should be deliberately left within Paddock Paradise on track. There are two reasons: *dominance* and *copraphagous* behaviors.

In the horse's natural world, social structure is based largely on *relative dominance* — that is, "pecking order". I will take this up again in a later section, but for now our purpose is served if we leave in place what are called "stud piles", a form of territorial marking that we see in the wild home range. These are signals to home range bands, and competitive bands visiting from outlying home ranges, to respect an alpha stud and his alpha female's territory. I recommend leaving or, if there is no alpha male present, creating one or two stud piles per Paddock Paradise — placed generally on the side closest to real or putative groupings of horses outside the track (e.g., a neighbors horses), or within the track if running multiple bands, or along simultaneous tracks (e.g, breeding operation). These possibilities are taken up later in the discussion of "Multi-Tracks".

The piles can be several feet wide and as high as 2 or 3 feet [#7, PP Template]! The alpha male in your track, if you have one, may contribute to and use them as territorial reminders, while the alpha female (again, if your "herd" has such a female[1]) leads other band members to them regularly. Hence they are significant, if not unique, catalysts for naturally inspired on-track movement. This may seem strange or foolish to some of us, but to horses it is serious business, and we should welcome and facilitate this opportunity to get and keep our horses going forward with utmost natural impulsion.

#7

PP Template

Horse owners may balk at the suggestion that we should stockpile dung where our horses live. Isn't dung, in fact, a source of harmful parasites, one might ask in protest? I would have thought so myself had I not seen wild horses (and domestic, too, on more than one occasion), the very young anyway, regularly nibbling and consuming dung found in the home range. This is called *copraphagous behavior* by wildlife biologists. As long as this is the case in the horse's natural world, then we cannot presume that it is harmful behavior, or somehow incidental or irrelevant in Paddock Paradise. Hence, we should not deprive domestic horses of the same opportunity. One approach would be to "rotate" old dung out of the track, while confining newer dung to areas immediately around the stud piles — assuming that there is even a significant build-up. Excess dung can be spread over adjacent pastures as a manure fertilizer, or selectively, in gardens either fresh or composted. At the AANHCP Field

---

[1] If your "herd" is all male, then an alpha male should emerge with a sub-dominant "Lieutenant" cross-gendering the alpha female's role. In other words, the wild model shows that hierarchy arises in all band configurations.

Headquarters, dung is pulverized on track using a "drag" pulled behind an ATV. Effectively rendered to dust, it is absorbed ("biodegrades") into the ground (quickly so following rain) or drifts into the inner pasture, where it fertilizes plantlife growing there. Whatever one does with the dung — kept or removed — do so effectively in relation to biodegradation, as well as dominance and copraphagous behaviors.

Rolling, Pawing, and Bathing Behaviors

There seem to be two distinct patterns of rolling behavior in wild horse country. One, as described earlier, is a "mud" bath and occurs in relation to the water hole, the other occurs elsewhere on track and is more of a "dusting" experience. The importance of these to the horse in his natural world is undeniable, and bands will "line up" to take turns ("relative dominance" once more at work!) where competition for the rolling site is underway.

The mud bath is really a warm weather phenomenon, as described in Chapter 1. We can expand our existing water hole to facilitate this important behavior [#8, PP Template]. Understanding how it occurs in the wild will guide us in its construction. Typically, an entire band enters the water to drink (regardless of temperature); group pawing behavior soon "drenches" band members, and rolling or "bathing" behavior soon ensues right in the water! This may last for several minutes (depending on competition or predator pressure). From the water, band members go immediately to the shore where they roll in the mud, dirt, (and sand) in effect coating themselves with "mud". I would liken the final effect to a "mud pack" seen in health spas with hot springs. Indeed, in the hot sun, the mud soon forms a "crust" upon the horse's coat. With subsequent movement on track, the crust breaks and reveals a beautiful, healthy coat — such as you can see in the many photos of wild horses in this book and my and other's written works about wild horses.[1]

Elsewhere on track, wild horses visit what I call

#8
§
PP Template

---

[1]For additional photos of the wild horse, visit the AANHCP website (www. aanhcp.net) and Facebook.

"dusting sites". Here, the ground is literally pulverized into fine dust by the countless "pawings" and "rollings" of bands visiting from many home ranges over unknown generations. In one spectacular showing, I witnessed over 50 horses standing in an immense circle awaiting their turns (by band, of course), a cloud of dust concealing and rising over the immediate participants, powdered faces strangely aghast like a mime trouper! Once more, as wind and movement conjoined to clear the dust, beautiful glistening coats were the product. But why such dedication to this behavior? A massage? Insect deterrence? An itch? All of these, perhaps.

I recommend some ingenuity here, creating your own dust site somewhere on or just off track, but away from the water hole [#9, PP Template] — we don't want this site used by wet horses! At this point, I don't know what to recommend for "dust" or even how to create it to elicit the rolling behavior we are seeking — but will welcome input from horse owners who are willing to experiment with possibilities and share their results with me to pass along to others in future editions of this book or my seminars. Depending on the soil conditions in your Paddock Paradise, the horses may do the best job of creating it themselves.

#9

PP Template

Camping Behaviors: Resting, Sleeping and Grooming

Whereas feeding behavior occupies the greatest portion of equine life in the wild, "camping" behavior assumes a not too distant second — roughly a third of his daily life.

By camping, I mean he's basically standing around, and movement on track has effectively come to a halt.

During the years I visited family bands (1982-1986), these frequent "camp outs" provided me with ample opportunity to appreciate the deeper, inner emotional life of these quintessential natural horses. There is no greater dread that could be imposed upon them than to physically separate them from their family units. Humans could well learn a lesson here! At regular intervals, family members take every opportunity to stop at favorite camp spots to rest or sleep, groom every reachable part of each other, form defensive circles with nose-to-nose breathing in the

comforting scent of one another, or to simply lay about without pressure in quiet repose. I have fallen into comforted deep sleep myself on more than one occasion in this familial setting with the sounds, smells and sights of equine wildness all around me.

Horses love to sleep. And in the wild, they lay down to do this. But it always seems that one is left standing, rear hoof cocked, a sentinel at half-sleep. Come night, family bands, two or more together (including a bachelor band), will camp on an open ridge top, plain, or forest meadow. And so it was on my very first night ever among them, camp was set, by the alpha mare and stallion, and, taking their cue, I decided this was as good a time as any to get some shut-eye myself. Laying down in my sleeping bag, I peered into the stars above waiting for the first shooting star to streak the sky, a habit I acquired among them and used to my advantage to create sleepy eyes. At half mast, however, I was suddenly jolted out of my bag like a Jack-in-the-Box by a deafening roar I can only liken to one of those dinosaurs in Jurassic Park! With my heart pounding away, and not knowing where it came from or from what source, I was blasted by a second trumpeting. It was the alpha stallion! I'd never heard a sound like it before among domestic horses. Within seconds, this calling out was greeted by distant similar trumpetings across the alluvial plains and ridges. I stood in amazement as this chorus of cacophony echoed seemingly everywhere for minutes before coming to a halt. And then silence. What I had witnessed was an equine GPS system of sorts. The alpha stallions were calling out their relative positions: "I am here. And I am over here. And I am here too. Etc." Ostensibly, this is to let each other know that all is well, and more importantly, that everyone is where they are supposed to be. An equine barometer of their contiguous spheres of intolerance.

§

"Mutual grooming" on track at the AANHCP Paddock Paradise as the marine layer from the nearby ocean shrouds the mountains. Not obvious here, the action was not one of chewing on their coats, but a left-right swiping of the gums across each other's backs. Natural gum/dental care in the works?

#10

PP Template

The "lesson from the wild" to apply here is that horses in Paddock Paradise should be expected and allowed to rest and sleep throughout the day. And, if there are competitive multi-bands on track, or segragated tracks, to expect and allow trumpeting in the night across Paddock Paradise. This is all "milling around" behavior. It isn't necessary for our horses to move constantly (and at that, slow walking) 24/7 to generate those beautiful hooves. Unlike dogs, but like domestic cats, I suppose, they prefer camping in different locations — favorite spots is how I would describe them. Accordingly, I would provide several enlarged areas for camping along the track. I recommend one in the forest [#10, PP Template] and another in the open elsewhere, preferably on high ground. Your horses may choose to camp elsewhere, in which case, enlarge those areas — always just room enough to fit everyone in there together comfortably. That electric fence is meant to be moved as necessary to "best fit" your unique Paddock Paradise.

Reproductive and Foaling Behavior

I decided to group reproductive and foaling behaviors under the "extraordinary" classification of the 95-5 Principle. The stress and strains of breeding, and the struggles of the newborn foal to gather and collect himself within minutes of birth to join his family on track, are nothing less than extraordinary. This discussion should be of interest to horse breeders, or anyone with a mare ready to foal, because Paddock Paradise provides the ideal environment for reproductive and foaling behaviors.

When mares enter estrus, and assuming that breeders have targeted specific mares and stallions for procreation, I recommend that a given breeding stallion and his mares (to be bred) be placed on one track, and all other males removed to a second track (e.g., a bachelor band). If more than one stallion is breeding, then they also should be situated on their own tracks and with their respective mares. These kinds of divisions, or separations, occur in the wild, and therefore, apply in Paddock Paradise. (Multi-track systems are discussed further later in this chapter.) The exception to the foregoing would be when alpha and sub-dominant breeding stallions are "buddies" and prefer to be on the same track, rather than separated in a multi-track configuration. This occurs in the wild too,[1] and should be facilitated in Paddock Paradise with discretion. Breeding in all cases may take place on track, or, in combination with "turnouts" off-track; I can't see that it will make any difference.

From the moment of birth, newborn foals should live their lives on track, moving with the normal "flow" of movement established by the alpha mares and alpha males (if present). Within hours of birth, foals are ready to

[1] Ibid., *TNH*, p. 23-26

go. This is as nature intended. Segregating foals from band members, including their fathers or surrogate male figures, in other words breaking down the equine family unit, is probably an invitation to aggressive or aberrated behaviors and generally unnatural socialization patterns. Paddock Paradise enables healthy social interaction by providing the right environment for horse families.

#11

—

PP Template

I recommend creating breakout cells — cul de sacs, if you will — from the track for foaling purposes [#11, PP Template]. In the wild, parturient mares leave the family unit to give birth alone — this is nature's way. Let us accommodate our domestic mares by affording them the same opportunity to "be alone" during birthing.

Family members will naturally adjust their movements on track to stay close by. I have witnessed first hand the powerful ties of mare-to-band during foaling, and the vigilance of others to stand down on track as the mare prepares and gives birth. This strong emotional connection does much to mitigate anxiety and stress that would otherwise leave the mare in isolation. Again, this is nature's way, and we must reach just a little to help. As this facet of Paddock Paradise is still in uncharted territory, I can only speculate that it may be necessary to accommodate family "camping" behavior during foaling by concentrating feed, water, and resting areas in close proximity to the birthing cell. I ask horse owners to employ their imaginations and report their successes to me for the sake of others.

For now, let us ensconce the birthing cell in the wooded area or some semi-secluded enclave affording the same effect in the mind of the horse. The area should be small enough for the mare to foal in, and possibly accommodate a second (beta) mare (e.g., an "aunt" or close buddy). Her role will be to help police the foaling area of intruders until the newborn has arrived and becomes mobile.

Agonistic and Play Behaviors

Agonistic behavior is combative behavior, simply put, a time to "fight". Play behavior, at least among the males, closely remsembles agonistic behavior. In the wild, male horses love to play fight, and the alpha stallions engage in serious combat in their competition for females in estrus. Females at play, or when feeling threatened, are more likely to strike or kick at unwanted intruders who come too close — outright combat appears to be limited to the males.

Let us afford our domestic horse on track the same opportunities to play *and* fight. Such behavior will do much to grind and shape the hooves, as well as build strong bodies — so this is an important dimension of Paddock Paradise, too. I recommend that horses be removed from their track and released into a large holding area, or even a pasture, for this purpose [#12, PP Template]. Perhaps the area circumscribed by the interior (electric) fence will serve this purpose.

#12
—
PP Template

I recommend that this be done daily, one or more times, and at your convenience. Instinctively, the horses will look forward to this opportunity whenever it is accorded them. Life on track automatically prepares them (as an extended "warm up") for what is going to follow — a rousing good time! Let all the horses in there at the same time. And once in there, follow this cardinal rule: no one, male or female, young or old, is allowed to stand around idly, and no one is allowed to eat or drink either. This is no time to give treats or "bond" with your horse. It's time for them to run, kick, fight, play — anything goes, as long as it is vigorous and extraordinary. If you want your horses to possess really naturally shaped hooves, this is the time to make them work for them.

Be creative in getting them to move thusly; if one is inclined to indolence, adding a more "frisky" equine pal may stimulate him to move! If fights break out, let them have at it. Let them kick, strike, bite, mount, scream, threaten, anything agonistic in nature. Let the dust fly, the turf rip. Since your horses are not in shoes, and the hooves have been trimmed with a "mustang roll",[1] you shouldn't have to worry about serious injuries. It's okay for them to take a battle scar or two (unless you are in show

---

[1] For a thorough description of the "mustang roll", see my book *The Natural Trim: Principles and Practice.*

season — although if I were a judge I would reward battle scars, especially on the males!). Garnering a limp now and then shouldn't be a cause for worry — it happens all the time in the wild, and everyone gets better just fine. This might also be a propitious time to mix those bands living in segregated multi-tracks — alpha stallions, in particular — to really mix it up. Of course, if you are harboring a rehab case, make allowances, although I want to see them having at it too if they are physically able. Don't be surprised if you find one of your hobbling rehab cases limp at high speed to take a crack at someone!

When the horses seem tired, it's time to open the gate and put them back on track. How long was this volatile turnout? Probably several minutes to half an hour (at most), depending on their conditioning. If you turn them out more than once a day, say morning and evening, then it might cut short a bit, depending on how long they were out the first time. Based on the 95-5 Principle, we can calculate approximate "on track" and "turn out" time frames:

24 hr. day   95% Ordinary Behavior (On track time)

5% Extraordinary Behavior (Off track time)

.95 (24 hr.)   .05 (24 hr.)

22.8 hrs.   1.2 hr. (72 min.)

In other words, they require about about an hour of reasonably vigorous turnout time per day. Remember, 5% is only an estimate. It could be less or more. On average, I would say turnout should be 45 minutes to an hour or slightly more per day. In other words, 20 to 30 minutes or so per turnout, twice a day. This is not to say that the horses can't go longer, or shouldn't go less, they can. This is simply a base-line figure for extraordinary behaviors to work from. Three 10 minute turnouts per day seems even better to me, as an hour of continuous vigorous activity is unusual, even by wild horse standards.

Always make allowances. This isn't intended to be a macho adaptation of the horse's natural world. Lame or infirm horses, senior horses, the very young, pregnant mares, even the lazy, will need latitude here. Horses in rigorous training, such as those competing in endurance riding, may prosper with more periods of turnout, or extended turnout times. Again, this is another uncharted territory of Paddock Paradise, and common sense should always reign until we have more data.

Equestrian Activities

A corollary of agonistic behavior is that equestrian activities may in some proportion be substituted for "at liberty" play and combat [#13, PP Template]. But not entirely. And here we must exercise caution: agonistic behavior is what it is, and unless the equestrian sport simulates such behavior, such as in the classical school of riding (airs, passage, piaffe, etc.), we may be robbing the horse of his native extraordinary locomotory requirements. Track racing and endurance riding, for example, even though extraordinary by all accounts, would not be suitable subsitutes for off-track turnout. They fail inclusively to serve the horse at his teleologic core.

#13

PP Template

Some equestrians may wonder what role "hot walkers" and "lungeing" may play in all of this. I am dubious that either have any value in the extracellular life of Paddock Paradise, except possibly lunging in very limited ways. Horses do not naturally go in circles for extended periods of time, as on the walker. They do go "well-collected" in small circles (for example, foals in play encircling their mothers) for short twirls, and thus lunging may have some value in the training and gymnasticizing of young horses in preparation for riding. Otherwise, life on track and at turnout should entirely supplant these two "devices" for exercising the horse.

§
Riding "off-track" in Paddock Paradise

In summary, while life on-track, and calculated turnout time off-track, certainly prepare the horse for most equestrian activities, the horse owners should make every effort to balance their riding agendas against the locomotive needs exemplified by the 95-5 Principle. This shouldn't be hard to do, and common sense once more should always reign to govern our final choices.

Prey/Predator Behavior

In the wild, many family bands must face the ubiquitous presence of feline and canine predators — the cougar, wolves, and coyotes. Cougars stalk and attack foals during the birthing season, roughly six months out of the year; hence, they contribute to the extraordinary behaviors we are seeking in accordance with the 95-5 Principle. Although this may seem a stretch for Paddock Paradise advocates, my feeling is that we should make an effort to build in a simulated threat. By way of analogy, pilots and astronauts are trained using simulators — giving students a sense of being in a real, albeit ersatz, command flight situation. I propose that we do this two ways: by sound and by scent,.

The idea here is to convince our horses that there is a predator threat, without, of course, subjecting them to the real thing. Game hunters use sounds and scents to attract their prey. Conversely, we need the scent of the cougar to incite our bands to defenesive and flight formations during on and off-track time — that is, to strike fear-based movement. These stimulants should be used judiciously, perhaps once or twice a month, so as not to dull the horse's senses of sound and smell. Commercial scents and recordings of cougars may already be available, if not then this is yet another project for the horse-using community to move on if Paddock Paradise is to operate full-bore and serve our horses' needs.

Continuing, horses do not need to see a facsimile cougar, which they would not be convinced by anyway. In the wild, they are alerted by sound and scent. When the attack comes, it is with such lightning speed that there is little band members can do to protect their young if they lie outside the mare's circle (discussed in Chapter 1). So

"seeing" the attacker isn't necessary, as much as sensing
her close proximity. With a little ingenuity, we can setup
a simulated pre-attack by subjecting band members
simultaneously to the cougar's scent and her roar [#14, PP
Template] — more on a sound system for doing this a little
later in this chapter. I suppose it wouldn't hurt also to
have an automated device in place that, at the same time,
flings some object at or near band members. This could be
fun! Remember, we are after fear-based movement here,
which also contributes to the grinding and shaping of the
hooves, and the general health of the horse through
diverse but natural extraordinary movement. If we
haven't challenged our horses in the name of a mountain
lion attack, then we have set our sights for success just
that much lower.[†]

Relative Dominance

Closely related to agonistic behavior, is *relative
dominance*, something I have described at length in my
books, *The Natural Horse* and *The Natural Trim*.[1] Horse
owners should review this material before proceeding
with their efforts to create Paddock Paradise. Briefly,
relative dominance is "pecking order" behavior. It is
natural and necessary for ordered movement on-track
such as we observe in the wild. This is an area of much
confusion among horse owners, so I want to labor it a bit
for the sake of achieving success in Paddock Paradise.

In the wild, horses form relationships based on relative
dominance and cooperation. As every human on the
planet isn't going to get along with everyone else, so it is
true in the world of horses. Our horses must be allowed to
choose their friendships, alliances, and relative positions
in the band's or herd's natural pecking order. This isn't
something we determine for them, they determine it
themselves.

For example, horses pick their positions on trail rides
with other horses. Horse owners who don't respect this
may get caught him in the middle of the ensuing not-so-
friendly jabs and nips that take place. Such competitive-

#14

—

PP Template
§

[†]No doubt, naysayers will
scoff at our #14 spur. Yet,
at the AANHCP Field
Headquarters, there are
cougars (and coyotes and
bears) inhabiting the
area, and the watchful
eyes and extraordinary
collection we see in our
family band no doubt re-
flects their prey instinct.
How about this as an al-
ternative — set up a dog
run at point #14, which
may facilitate a "chase"
sequence, if your dog is
given to such play. The
effect should be the same,
if the set-up is done effectively. Worth a try!

---

[1]Ibid.. *TNH, pp.* 19-21 and 148-149; *TNT,* pp. 160-167.

dominance behavior may blow up into outright agonistic behavior, which is dangerous to the riders stuck in the middle, and can easily result in human broken bones if the horses decide to kick each other. I understand that at the famed Spanish Riding School (Vienna, Austria), young Lippizan stallions are brought to the school's riding hall and turned loose together to spar and establish their hierarchies (pecking orders) based on relative dominance. These orders are pivotal in the instructors' decisions to match horse-and-rider according to each partner's temperament, and position during training and performances. As basically the same thing holds true in the wild, this is what we must also facilitate in Paddock Paradise.

#15

—

PP Template

Probably the best place to work out relative dominance is during off-track, turnout time. This may take every minute and more of the allotted time for band/herd members to work out their pecking order. Be prepared for skirmishes and combat, as this is the way it works [#15, PP Template]. I can't imagine that a peaceful, "harmonic convergence" will take place, but if it does, I would be inclined to "borrow" another horse who can stir things up. We want the band's natural leaders (alpha mare and alpha male) to emerge. As in the wild, expect a mare to "lead" and a male to "drive" the band forward on-track. As rivalries distill into well-defined pecking order "positions", life on-track will settle into the realm of ordinary behaviors in keeping with the 95-5 Principle. Once more, I advise horse owners not to interfere with the off-track "sorting" that's going to take place. Let the horses work it out among themselves, as they always will when we don't project our own misconceptions of social order and acceptable behavior into their world.

Texturing the Track with Terrain, Sounds, and Smells

I described the use of terrain, sounds, and smells (e.g., scents) in fleshing out Paddock Paradise. Let's discuss these further when an eye to the basic template — design and architecture — of the track.

Terrain

I believe the terrain through which the track passes should be as interesting and diverse as we can make it. If sections of your land are convoluted, if it has a stream or a pond, is wooded, rocky, whatever, direct the track into those areas. We want the horse to work his body and his feet. "Flat land" will work too, but not as efficiently as land that is rugged or is at least "textured" to simulate the Great Basin environment. Indeed, texturing the track is something that most of us can now afford to do — we no longer have to concern ourselves with working the entire property, which would probably break most pocketbooks, anyway.

So, don't stick just to the perimeter of your property in laying out your track. Depending on the lay of your land and the amount of land you can put to use, you could run interesting "veins" — alternate trails leaving one part of the track and re-entering at another point further along — to pick up a stream, pond, gravel bed, and other diverse features [#16, PP Template]; and "spurs" — short trails leading from the main track to useful cells, such as the dusting area(#9, PP Template). Use your imagination, but in so doing orchestrate the innovations so that band movements are not stymied or reversed, but continue generally forward.

I also like the idea of creating a track such that it would be difficult for a horse standing in one location to see a horse elsewhere — except at a distance. In the horse's "curious" frame-of-mind, this translates to "keep moving" to see what's happening up ahead; in his "familiar" state-of-mind, it means let's get to the next familiar thing to eat, see, or smell.

#16

PP Template

Consider texturing short, separate stretches of the track with logs or large branches, gravel (use crushed and tamped/rolled surfacing like a rural county road), sand,

and other abrasive materials [#17, PP Template]. If the horses refuse to pass over them, then it is probably too much, too soon for their hooves and minds to adapt to. Horses must be given time to transition and adapt to the track, and strategically, we should bear this in mind. What they may not be able to do today, at the outset, they will probably be able to do weeks or months down-line through progressive conditioning. Plan your track

AANHCP horses skirt the perimeter of the inner pasture — a founder trap for horses. Use "veins" and "spurs" to lengthen, enhance and diversify your track system in Paddock Paradise.

accordingly, by graduating the track's abrasiveness over time. You can do test runs by diverting your horses into short veins or spurs and see how they do.

Horses will need flat areas on-track for camping. I recommend that you provide shade and a wind break in these areas — trees, a shelter, etc. [#18, #10, PP Template]. They may decide also to hold-up in these campsites during spells of inclement weather, such as an ice-storm. They will know instinctively what to do, where to stay, and how long to remain there. Throw feed in these campsites only until the weather hazard has passed; then don't feed there again (or until another weather hazard erupts).

Feeding long term in campsites imprints feeding behavior in association with stationary (e.g., resting) behavior. Which is unnatural and and conditions the horse to "eat in place" — in other words, it fosters unmotivated equine behavior and weak hooves.

#18

PP Template

Sounds

For very little investment, you can string a speaker system around your track, and wire it to a simple sound system through which you can play sounds that are "music to the ears" of horses. As an advocate of the natural horse, I would encourage interested parties to record the sounds of wild horse country and market them as CDs for Paddock Paradise. These sounds should correspond to the behaviors and sounds heard in wild horse country. I have identified some of these in earlier pages of this book — stallion bellowings in the night, the roar of cougars [#14, PP Template], the sound of the wind in the junipers, and so forth. While these may seem meaningless, irrelevant, or even ludicrous to our way of thinking, they are teleogical reminders of the horse's natural world which will serve us as stimulants for natural movement. By way of analogy, people often buy CDs of ocean sounds for the imagery and feelings they elicit. I will personally work with anyone who wishes to take it upon themselves to record such sounds and make them available commercially to horse owners for use in Paddock Paradise.

Smells

Wild horse country is replete with the smells of the natural horse's world. I have mentioned the scent of the cougar earlier as an impetus for prey/predator based movement. We can use this in Paddock Paradise, along with others: trees, plants, herbs, flowers, mineral deposits, rolling areas, and so forth. Commercial possibilities abound here, as with the CD mentioned above for sounds. Interested horse owners may wish to visit wild horse country on their next vacation to see what can be identified and duplicated for this purpose. Check with the BLM for potential land use regulations.

Complementary Animals

Wild horse country, in addition to the mustang, is full of domestic livestock and varied wildlife. I believe a symbiosis based on complementary feeding behavior is at work between the different species, and one we can put to work for us in Paddock Paradise.[1,2] I've mentioned earlier that the green grass pasture that some readers may have within the electric fence perimeter, is potentially hazardous to the horse — specifically, it is a known laminitis trigger. Some people are disc plowing the track to suppress grass, or are using chemical grass killers to control growth. Alternatively, put other grazers in with your horses to help get rid of the grass. Cattle, sheep, llamas, goats, and scarabs (dung harvesters) come to mind. Goats should be very suitable for smaller operations, and you can remove them to elsewhere when they are no longer needed [#19, PP Template]. They will naturally keep their distance from the horses, sweeping up the trail ahead, or cleaning up from behind. Count on them to eat anything in there, though, so guard or remove your herb flats while the goats are on-track.

Veterinary Care

#19

—

PP Template

Due to the horse's strong sense of smell, I would discourage veterinary care inside Paddock Paradise. Vets bring with them the odoriferous chemicals of their trade, and this is bound to collide with and negatively disrupt the natural, and holistic biodynamics of the track. Recalling the "no human allowed" clause of the Paddock Paradise paradigm, horse owners are encouraged to remove their horses from the track before the vet arrives, returning them after he or she has left the property altogether.

[1]Ibid., *HOG,* see discussion in Introduction.

[2]Ibid., Marlow, et al. discuss forage competition.

In Pursuit of Equine Vitality

From 2011 until 2017, a Paddock Paradise experiment was undertaken at the AANHCP Field Headquarters near Lompoc, California along the state's central coast. Four horses — three geldings and one mare — were put on track, with an additional mare added a little over a year later. The track extended up a mountainside, forming a half mile loop on the ridge top, with another half mile loop extending down to their water trough, a mile long in total. The ground, with the exception of a "sand pit" for rolling, was almost entirely gravel. The climate is arid, in fact, very similar to the high desert biome of the U.S. Great Basin. In short, the AANHCP Paddock Paradise promised — and delivered — the very benefits based on the wild horse model I've discussed throughout this book.

Paddock Paradise
AANHCP Field Headquarters
Lompoc, CA (USA)

Being a professional "hoof man", I've always gauged the success of any hoof care regimen — or care management regime, in general — by the health and soundness of the horse and his feet. Either the regimen works, or it doesn't. And so this was the standard to which I held the holistic care practices of the AANHCP Field Headquarters. Those of us involved were able to demonstrate that Paddock Paradise not only delivers equine vitality, but brings us to the very threshold of the wild horse model upon which Paddock Paradise is based. On the pages that follow are a short photo essay of our horses and their lives during their stay in our Paddock Paradise (see image key on facing page).

The decision to completely revamp this book, and simply lay out what we did at the AANHCP Field Headquarters was rejected because the story behind Paddock Paradise needs to be told, and because the basic template and "lessons from the wild" described are fundamentally correct and timelessly applicable. The AANHCP Paddock Paradise, in fact, is only one possibility. Today, ten years

(Continued on page 140)

My colleague and fellow board member of the AANHCP Jill Willis and I are visiting and inspecting the track, as we do daily. Our late official mascot, "Shelby" joins us! Join us too on this "official" tour!

Our horses appear from behind a hill on full alert — strangers (that could be you!)

have entered their home range and its time for a full investigation!

The horses gather at one of five "feed stations" spaced along our one mile long

track. At each station hay bags are strung from poles. Each horse gets their own bag, but sharing is common within the family band.

This is the "upper" track, viewed from NW to SE; Santa Barbara mountains lie in the distance. The track surrounds an eight acre field, which the horses cannot en-

ter due to the presence of a low voltage electric fence which is turned off 99% of the time!

Fog ("marine layer") weaves through the gulch below, while the horses feed at one

of the uppermost feed stations. Eating frequently is natural to the horse and important for their digestion.

This view is taken from above our Paddock Paradise in the opposing direction

seen on pages 128-129. Note lush green grasses.

Same view as previous page spread, showing the clash of seasons, the pasture now

dry and arid.

The horses ascend one of the steeper inclines on the track on their way to the highest point
in our Paddock Paradise, 600 feet above the lowest point of the track. They will make this

journey from top to bottom numerous times during the day. Such locomotive behavior has given them athletic bodies and hooves of "steel".

Another view from above as an early winter storm approaches our Paddock Paradise. The dry grass will come alive and flourish until early spring. It is important that the horses not

enter the track during this time as grass has been implicated in the hoof disease known as laminitis.

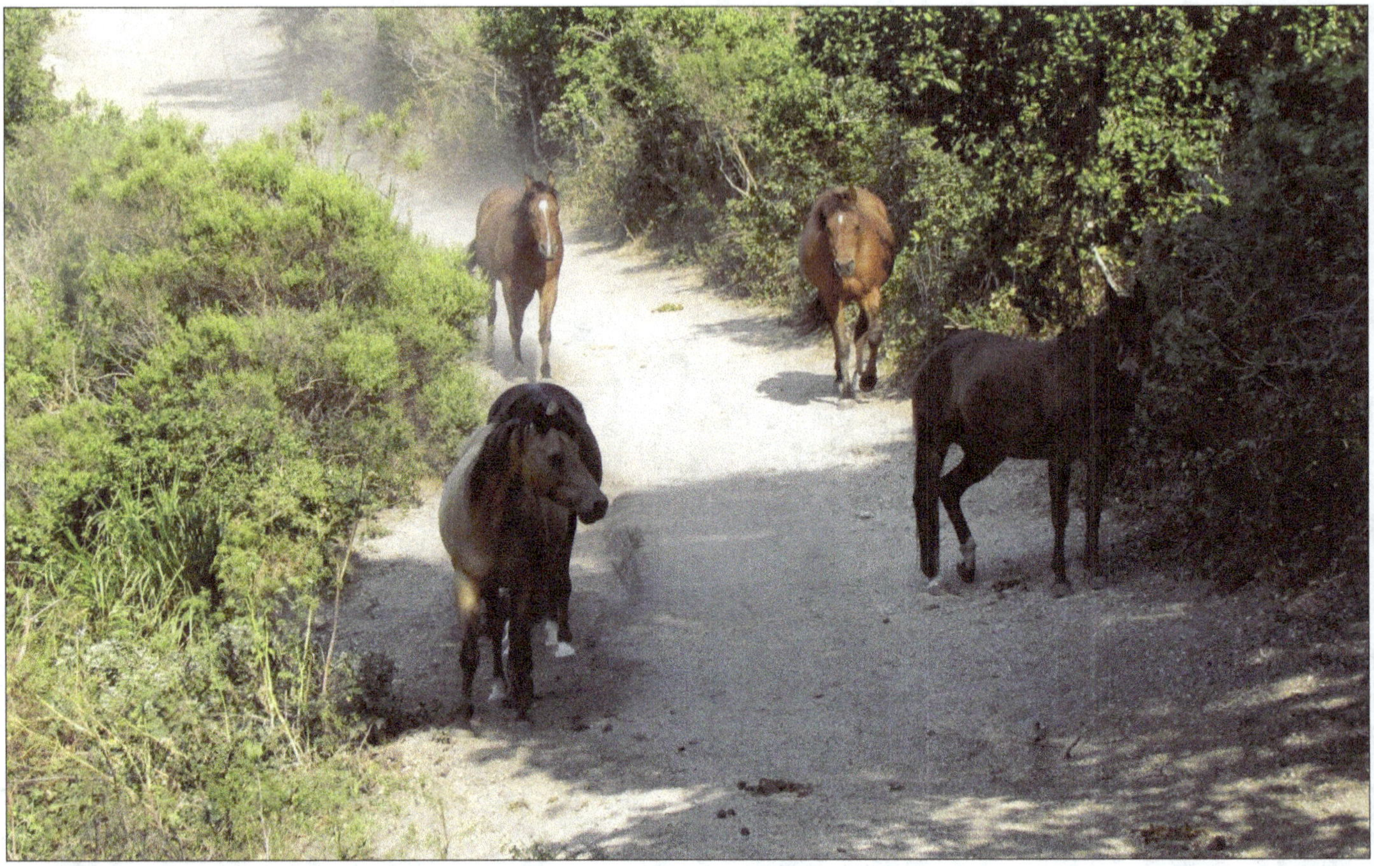

(Top) The horses have left the upper track descending the steepest path in our Paddock Paradise. (Below). The horses have gathered together at the "sand pit" where they will roll and sleep for an hour or more. As seen here, one or more horses will stand vigilant as other members fall into deep sleep.

On many hillsides adjacent to their track, the horses will harvest many vital nutrients from plants and rocks. (Top) Here, one of the horses has "pawed" the ground open to get at a root. (Below) Branches and foliage are eaten.

As the midday suns bears down, the horses seek relief in the shade provided by a run-in shelter. They may also go here during a winter rain storm. In either case, they are just as

often found cruising their track in complete indifference to the weather.

The horses take water in a winter rain fed pond.

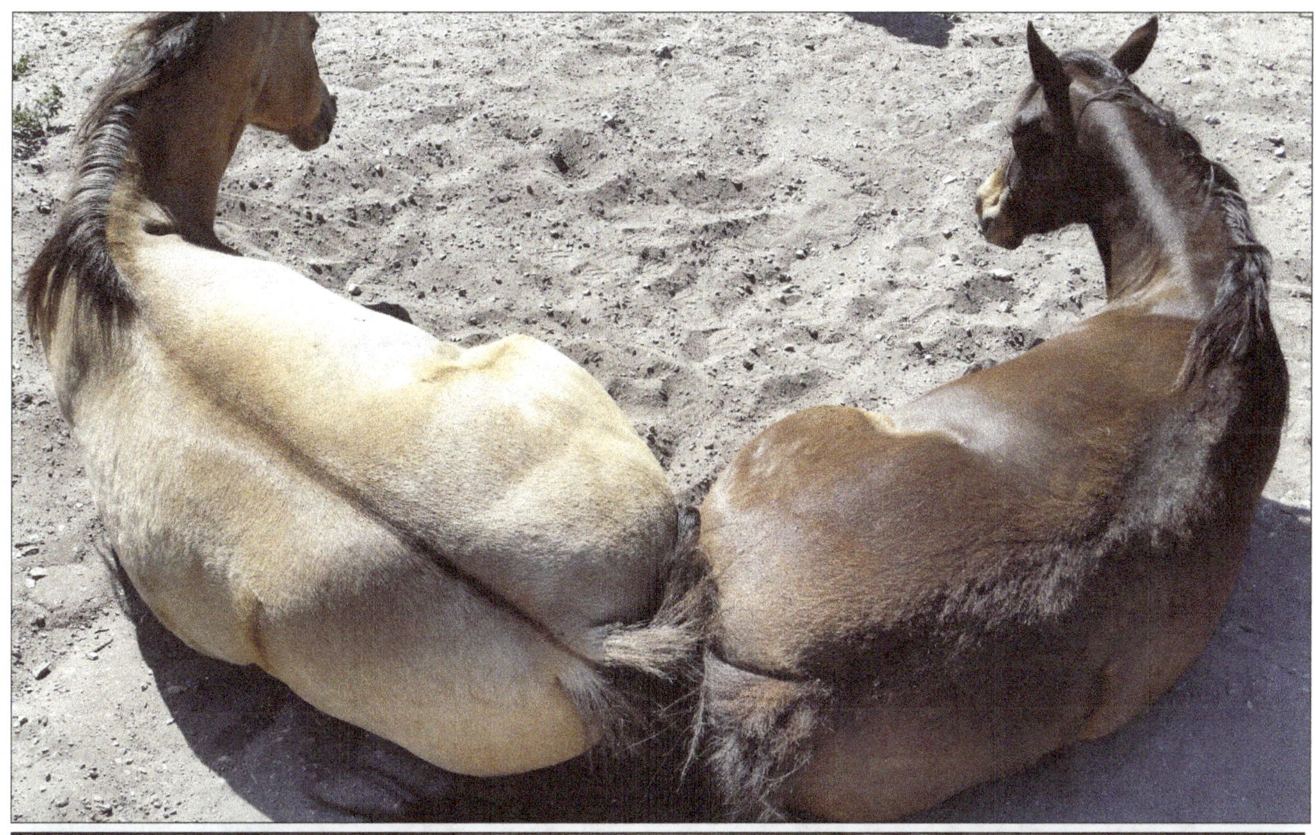

(Top) Two of the horses form equine "bookends" during a nap. (Below) In a moment the band will ascend the upper track for more hay, then just as quick return to the lower track as they are doing here.

At regular monthly intervals I checked the horses' hooves to see if they need trimming. (Above) I am inspecting a hoof with a fellow veteran AANHCP trimmer. (Below) I'm finishing a hoof in what we call the "4th Position of the Natural Trim" — the same limb position an angry horse will deploy for play sparring or fight kicking other horses (and obnoxious people too!). I have plied this trade for over forty years, first as a farrier and later as the world's first "natural hoof care practitioner".

Naturally worn hooves in our Paddock Paradise.

(Top and below) Rolling behavior is extremely important to the horse, in both the wild and here in our Paddock Paradise. Rolling toughens the skin and conditions their coats.

(Top and below) Homeostatic forces act upon our horses through a specialized ad-aptation to create winter and summer coats.

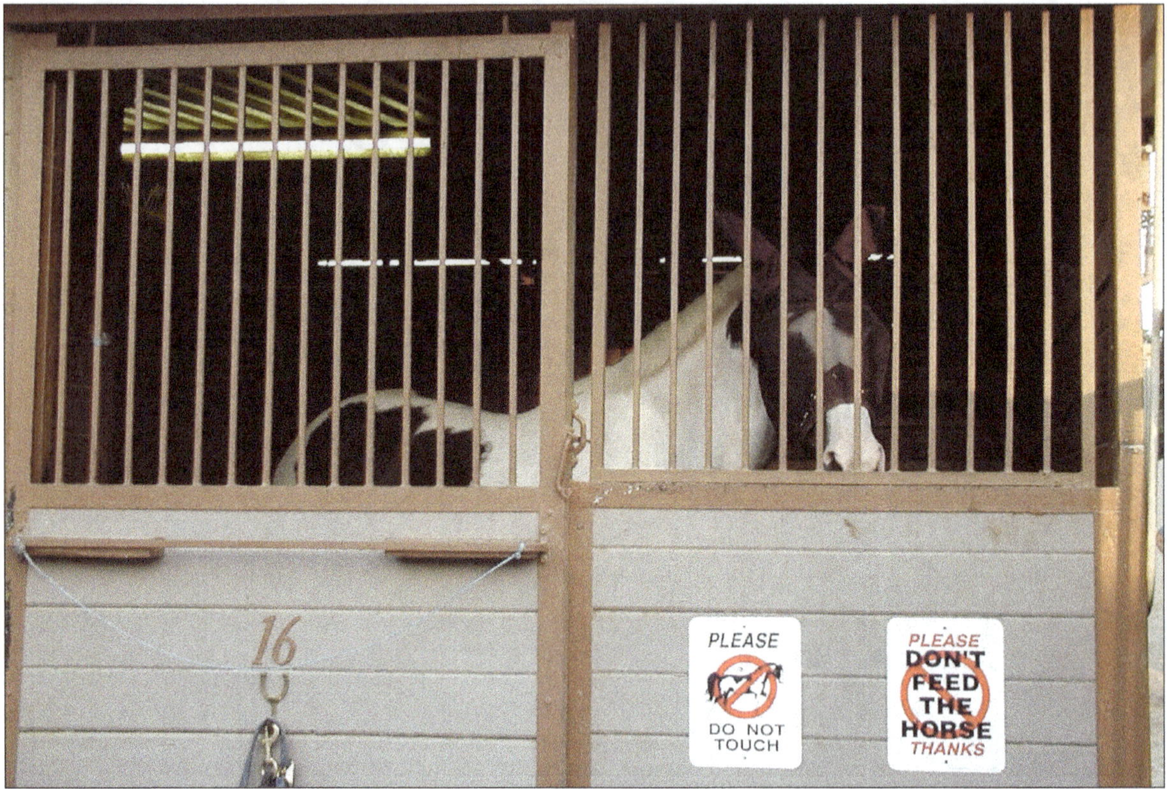

(Top and below) Reminders of the tragic clash between the horse's natural state and what amount to torturous equine isolation cages. Paddock Paradise bridges the gap, propelling the horse into a humane lifestyle fully "sanctioned" by nature!

(Above) I join the horses at a feed station in the early days of creating our Paddock Paradise. I am inspecting a sampling of new types of hay bags. These bags are a crucial component of the tracking system, enabling us to deliver hay to the horses that would otherwise be trampled, soiled, or blown away if fed on the ground. (Below) On their many daily rounds, the horses are searching out native plants and minerals to augment their diet.

(Top and below) Once a week I bring out the Ranger UTV and "drag" to keep grass marginalized on the fence line and the center pasture away from the track altogether.

(Salt licks are put out in several places along the track. At this Feed Station, they are slung from two of the hay poles right along with the hay bags.

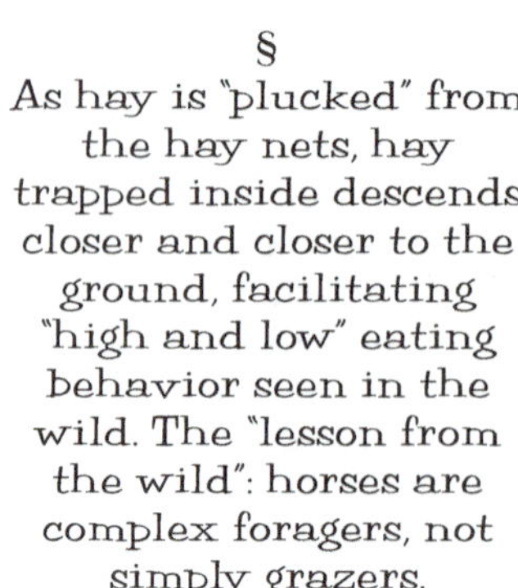

(Continued from page 108)

after *Paddock Paradise* was published, countless horse owners have taken the concept and made it work for their horses in a range of biomes. This is what I had hoped for.

The reader is invited to the new Paddock Paradise website (www.paddockparadise.net) to see what horse owners around the world are doing with this important concept. So go check it out! Many photographs and videos pepper the ongoing dialogues (in many languages!) as people share ideas and continue to develop their tracks. Indeed, the very concept of Paddock Paradise so resonates with the highest ideals of "natural boarding" that the sky is the limit in what might be done. With the wild horse model to keep us all in check and serving, as it does, as a vast resource for ideas, it really comes down to human ingenuity to make the most of the "lessons from the wild".

If you are new to the Paddock Paradise concept, and perhaps this book is the first you've heard of it, then I encourage you to think of your horse and what it can do for him in the best of ways. None of us has to own horses. So, to my way of thinking as an advocate, it is incumbent upon each of us to do what is best, humanely so, for our

horses. They are completely dependent upon us, and we
alone — as their trusted gaurdians — must make the
right decisions to help secure their well-being in today's
complicated world. Don't they deserve this? They are
amazing animals who have served our own species for
thousands of years, and whose genetic history is seemingly as timeless as the earth itself. Paddock Paradise,
rooted in the wild horse model, connects the horse both
in spirit and in flesh, and in the best of ways imaginable,
to his ancient past and uncorrupted vitality.

Jaime Jackson
Lompoc, CA
2018

NHC Resources

www.AANHCP.net
Association for the Advancement of
Natural Horse Care Practices

www.ISNHCP.net
Institute for the Study of Natural Horse Care Practices

www.jaimejackson.com

www.paddockparadise.net

NHC Facebook Pages
AANHCP · ISNHCP · Paddock Paradise
J. Jackson NHC Services · The Natural Trim

Image Credits

Cover
- (Front) Lisa Johnson
- (Back) Jill Willis

P.5
- Jim Hansen

P.6
- Kmusser

P. 9
- Jim Hansen

P. 10
- Jaime Jackson

P. 11
- Jaime Jackson

P. 12
- Jill Willis

P. 14-15
- Jaime Jackson

P. 10
- Jim Hansen

P. 18
- Illustration/track: Jaime Jackson & Milt Frei, U.S. Bureau of Land Management (BLM)
- Jim Hansen

P. 19
- Jaime Jackson

P. 20
- Jim Hansen

P. 21
- BLM

P. 22
- Jim Hansen

P. 23
- Asa Nuttal

P. 24
- Jim Hansen

P. 25
- Jaime Jackson

P. 27
- Jim Hansen

P. 29
- (Top) Jim Hansen
- BLM

P. 30
- Jim Hansen

P. 31
- BLM

P. 32
- Jim Hansen

P. 33
- Jim Hansen

P. 34-35
- Jim Hansen

P. 36
- Jim Hansen

P. 37
- Jim Hansen

P. 38
- BLM

P. 39
- Jim Hansen

P. 40
- Jaime Jackson

P. 41
- Jaime Jackson
- Jim Hansen

P. 42-43
- John Fitch

P. 44
- Jim Hansen

P. 45
- Jim Hansen

P. 47
- Jim Hansen

P. 48
- BLM

P. 49
- Jim Hansen

P. 50-51
- Jim Hansen

P. 55
- BLM
- BLM Wranglers: Jaime Jackson

P. 56
- Mark Jeldness

P. 57
- Mark Jeldness

P. 58
- Mark Jeldness

P. 59
- Mark Jeldness

P. 60-61
- Jaime Jackson

P. 62
- Jim Hansen

P. 63
- Neil Lockhart © www.123rf.com

P. 64
- Jill Willis

P. 69-70
- Jaime Jackson

P. 71
- Jaime Jackson
- Jill Willis

P. 72-73
- Jim Hansen

P. 74-75
- Jim Hansen

P. 76
- C.B. Marlow, et al.

P. 78-79
- Jaime Jackson

P. 80
- Jill Willis

P. 81
- Jill Willis

P. 83
- Marie & Senter Jackson

P. 88
- Jill Willis

P. 89
- Jill Willis

P. 90
- Marie & Senter Jackson

P. 91
- Marie & Senter Jackson

P. 95
- Marie & Senter Jackson

P. 100
- Jill Willis

P. 101
- Jill Willis

P. 102-103
- Jill Willis

P. 104
- Jill Willis

P. 107
- Derrick Neill © www.123rf.com

P. 108
- Jaime Jackson

P. 109
- Luke Tanner

P. 110-111
- Jill Willis

P. 112-113
- Jill Willis

P. 114-115
- Jaime Jackson

P. 116-117
- Jaime Jackson

P. 118-119
- Jaime Jackson

P. 120-121
- Jill Willis

P. 122-123
- Jill Willis

P. 124-125
- Jaime Jackson

P. 126-127
- Jill Willis

P. 128-129
- Jaime Jackson

P. 130
- Jaime Jackson

P. 131
- Jaime Jackson
- Erika Hopper

P. 132-133
- Jill Willis

P. 134-135
- Jill Willis

P. 136
- Jaime Jackson
- Jim Hansen

P. 137
- Luke Tanner
- Jill Willis

P. 138
- Jaime Jackson
- Sandra Satterthwaite

P. 140
- Jill Willis

P. 143
- Jill Willis

About the Author

aime Jackson is a maverick thinker and doer, never satisfied with life's limits in the mainstream. His calling is "nature" and what we can learn as a species from our natural world. After leaving the U.S. Army in early 1970, Jackson trained as a farrier (horseshoer). But from the beginning he was never happy with the pernicious effects of nailing shoes on the hooves of horses. This disillusionment led him in 1982 to America's wild horses roaming freely and undisturbed by the tens of thousands in the remote western lands of the Great Basin. "I found what I was looking for, nature's 'perfect' solution for what troubled me. There was nothing else to do but return to civilization and reveal what I found to whomever would listen — sound, healthy hooves perfectly shaped by the forces of nature." Jackson visited the horses over the next four years, an experience culminating in his first book, *The Natural Horse: Lessons from the Wild* (1992, Northland Publishing), a groundbreaking treatise on the natural state of the horse based on first hand experience.